Information Security Risk Management

Handbook for ISO/IEC 27001

Information Security Risk Management

Handbook for ISO/IEC 27001

Edward Humphreys

First published in the UK in 2010

by
BSI
389 Chiswick High Road
London W4 4AL

Typeset in Caslon Pro and Franklin Gothic by Monolith – http://www.monolith.uk.com
Printed in Great Britain by Berforts, www.berforts.co.uk

British Library Cataloguing in Publication Data
A catalogue record for this book is available from the British Library

ISBN 978-0-580-60745-5

Contents

This book is dedicated to my father, Thomas Edward Humphreys, and my mother, Alice Theresa (Stewart) Humphreys, and also to my sons Alexander, Thomas and James, and of course Anji.

I would like to thank all those reviewers, Dale Johnstone, Dr Angelika Plate, Dick Price and John Snare for their suggestions and invaluable comments.

Edward Humphreys

1 Introduction

1.1 Importance of risk management

Organizations, governments, society and citizens face many threats and risks. No one in these four broad groups is excluded from the situation. In addition we, as individuals, are both risk takers and risk averse depending on the particular circumstances we are in. We may take risks in one area of our lives and be risk averse in another area.

Modern society is highly dependent on the use of IT for commercial and private use. IT presents us with a variety of risks. As individuals we take risks and we are at risk: what we do, how we do things, and how we interact with the IT we use and the environment in which we live and work. There are also specific categories of risk – for example, physical and environmental risks, safety risks, health risks, financial risks, operational risks and, of course, information security risks.

Information is a business asset with varying levels of commercial value and sensitivity. In addition, some of this information is personal data. This means that information needs to be protected from the risk of being stolen, misused, modified, destroyed, or not being available to those authorized to have use of such information.

Information security is now a mainstream political, economic, societal and business issue. It is no longer the province of technologists alone; it is a far broader issue affecting all from the CEO, the company board, shareholders, senior and middle management through to every user and member of staff in the organization, irrespective of rank or job role.

1.2 Risk focused strategy

To be meaningful to the organization, a strategy for dealing with information security risks must be considered in a business context, and the interrelationships with other business functions – such as human resources, research and development, production and operations, administration, IT, finance and customers – need to be identified, to achieve a holistic and complete picture of these risks. This should include taking account of the organizational risks, and applying the concepts and ideas of corporate governance. This, together with the organization's business, effectiveness and the legal and regulatory environment, all serve as drivers and motivators for a successful risk management process. These ideas are explored in more detail in Chapter 3.

This book is focused on the concept of having an information security management system (ISMS) as the framework for achieving the effective management of information security risks. The international standard ISO/IEC 27001 is the world-recognized standard for establishing, implementing, monitoring and reviewing, updating and improving an ISMS.

This book is aimed at those business managers and their staff involved in ISMS risk management activities as a practical handbook for ISO/IEC 27005:2009 and ISO/IEC 27001:2005. It provides guidance and advice specifically to support the implementation of those requirements defined in ISO/IEC 27001:2005 that relate to risk management processes and associated activities. Many of the definitions used in this book are aligned with the generic risk standard ISO 31000:2009.

These ISO/IEC standards have adopted the process approach for assessing and treating risks, ongoing risk monitoring, risk reviews and reassessments. A process approach encourages users to take into account the importance of:

- understanding business information security requirements and the need to establish policy and objectives for information security;

- selecting, implementing and operating controls in the context of managing an organization's overall business risks;

- monitoring and reviewing the performance and effectiveness of the ISMS to manage the business risks;

- continual improvement based on objective risk measurement.

1.3 Risk process

This risk management process focuses on providing the business with an understanding of risks to allow effective decision-making to be applied to control the risks. The risk management process is an ongoing activity that aims to continuously improve the efficiency and effectiveness of the organization's ISMS implementation.

The risk management process should be applied to the whole ISMS (as specified in ISO/IEC 27001:2005) – that is, all elements of the ISMS. The process needs to be applied at the planning and design stages as well as the subsequent stages of operational deployment, monitoring and review of the risks, and the updating and improvement stages to ensure that any information security risks are always being appropriately managed.

An important part of the risk management process is the assessment of information security risks. This is necessary to understand the business information security requirements, and the risks to the organization's business assets. In ISO/IEC 27001:2005, the risk assessment includes the following actions and activities, which are described in more detail in Chapter 4:

- identification of assets;

- identification of legal and business requirements that are relevant for the identified assets;

- valuation of the identified assets, taking account of the identified legal and business requirements and the impacts of a loss of confidentiality, integrity and availability;

- identification of significant threats to, and vulnerabilities of, the identified assets;

- assessment of the likelihood of the threats and vulnerabilities to occur;

- calculation of risk;

- evaluation of the risks against a predefined risk scale.

The next step in the risk management process is to identify the appropriate actions to be taken for the treatment of each of the risks that have been identified during the risk assessment. Risks can be managed through a combination of prevention and detection controls, avoidance tactics, insurance and/or simple acceptance. Once a risk has been assessed, a business decision needs to be made on what, if any, action should be taken. In all cases, the decision should be based on a business case which justifies the decision and which can be accepted or challenged by key stakeholders. The different risk treatment options and factors that influence this decision are described in Chapter 5.

Once the risk treatment decisions have been made and the controls that were selected following these decisions have been implemented, the ongoing risk management activities should start. These activities include the process of monitoring the risks and the performance of the ISMS to ensure that the implemented controls work as intended. A further activity is risk review and reassessment, which is necessary to adapt the risk assessment to the changes that may occur over time in the business environment. Risk reporting and communication is necessary to ensure that business decisions are taken in the context of an organization-wide understanding of risks. The co-ordination of the different risk-related processes should ensure that the organization can operate in an efficient and effective way. Continual improvement is an essential part of the ongoing risk management activities to increase the effectiveness of the implemented controls towards achieving the goals that have been set for the ISMS. The ongoing risk management activities are described in Chapter 7.

The successful implementation of the risk management process requires that roles and responsibilities are clearly defined and discharged within the organization. Roles and responsibilities that are involved in the risk management process are included in ISO/IEC 27005, as relevant.

This Handbook gives guidance to support the requirements given in ISO/IEC 27001:2005 and the advice given in ISO/IEC 27005, regarding all aspects of an ISMS risk management cycle. This cycle includes assessing and evaluating the risks, implementing controls to treat the risks, monitoring and reviewing the risks, and maintaining and improving the system of risk controls.

1.4 Target audience

This Handbook is intended to be applicable to all organizations, regardless of their type, size and nature of business. It is intended for those business managers and their staff involved in ISMS risk management activities. It would also be useful for training and educational purposes and to anyone with an interest in the risk management aspects of ISO/IEC 27001:2005.

2 Nature of the Information Security Risk Landscape

2.1 Risk – what is it?

2.1.1 Definitions

Giving a definition of risk is difficult given the wide variety of ways in which the term is used and applied to different fields and applications. What is generally common to these different uses is that the context usually considers:

- uncertainty; and

- undesirable consequences.

For the purposes of interpreting the term 'information security risk' as it is used in this book we shall use the following definition:

> **Risk** = combination of the risk of exposure and the impact = combination of (likelihood of the threat being able to expose an element(s) of the system) and impact
>
> **Risk of exposure** is the likelihood that an element of the system lacks enough protection to be able to counter the effects of a threat. In other words, there is a likelihood that the system element is exposed to being at risk.

The *uncertainty* is that the organization can only estimate how likely it is to experience the risk of exposure; it cannot work on a basis of certainty. The *undesirable consequence* is the impact to which the organization may be subjected if its assets are exposed to risks. Here we have an important link between the impact and the value of the assets at risk.

The 'likelihood' is used to obtain estimates based on unknown parameters and on known outcomes. Therefore, in the risk definition above it is the 'likelihood' that the threats (unknown parameters) might be able to exploit weaknesses in the organization, to cause a risk of exposure. Sometimes the word 'probability' is used as a synonym for 'likelihood', particularly in non-technical everyday speech. However, there are technical and mathematical differences between 'likelihood' and 'probability': 'probability' allows us to predict unknown outcomes based on known parameters whereas 'likelihood' is based on unknown parameters and on known outcomes.

CASE STUDY EXAMPLES

1. Asset = Company sensitive information on future investments

This information is likely to be extremely valuable for the future of the company. Therefore, if it were to be lost, stolen or severely damaged in any way, the impact might be devastating for the future of the company, its financial state, its position in the market and its market shares and profits.

2. Asset = Customer personal data

This information is likely to be extremely important to the customers and might also be very sensitive. Therefore, if it were to be lost, stolen or severely damaged in any way, the impact might be devastating for both customers and the company. The company could suffer legal action, damage to its reputation and loss of customer confidence leading to customers taking their business elsewhere to a competitor. Similarly, to the customer there may be several impacts including financial loss as well as personal damage to the individual's standing, image and so on.

3. Asset = Company funds

These funds are of financial importance to the organization; therefore, if these funds were to be stolen through fraudulent activities, this would have a direct impact on company finances and might involve legal or regulatory action.

2.1.2 A world of risk

We live and work in a world in which society and the environment around us is inherently at risk. Nothing is certain in life and as a society we need to live with this fact. We cannot afford to be complacent and take the attitude 'it will never happen to us'. On the other hand, it is not wise to live in constant fear. We must take a balanced view and a sensible and measured approach to protecting what is important. Whatever we do to protect ourselves, we still cannot be certain that it will never happen. Even with protection there are no guarantees; there is always a residual risk to contend with. Protecting your car with the latest anti-theft devices does not mean that the vehicle will never be stolen as any protection is never 100 per cent foolproof; there will always be residual weaknesses in the system and, hence, there will always be residual risk. This is true for everything: medicines, IT, food safety, transportation safety, natural disasters, and so on.

Benjamin Franklin once said: 'There are only two things we can be certain of: death and paying taxes.'

So, in essence, risk management activities deal with the uncertainties and how we are able to manage, control and protect our business from the many risks and negative impacts that these uncertainties can cause. There are, of course, certain business activities and operations over which an organization can exercise more control than others, such as internal activities, whereas the organization has less influence, and hence control, over external factors – such as market conditions, the economic and political climate, competition and globalization.

2.1.3 Risk attitudes

A risk to one person might be an opportunity for another person. All humans have a risk attitude: they are risk seekers/risk takers, risk neutral or risk averse to certain things or activities. This attitude can be related to the behaviour of consumers, managers and investors in how they react to uncertainty. Which of these attitudes people adopt depends upon their perception of what is at stake, whether they will win or lose, whether they will be harmed or will be safe, whether they have a fear of taking the risk or they have no problem with taking a chance.

For example, a person is given the choice between two options, one certain and one uncertain. With the uncertain option, the person would need to take a gamble with an equal probability between receiving £100 or nothing. The alternative option is that the person would receive a specific amount of cash with certainty that is a probability of 1:

1. The risk-averse person would accept a certain payment of less than £50 (for example, £40) rather than take a gamble.

2. The risk-neutral person is nonchalant or unconcerned between taking the gamble and a certain £50 payment.

3. The risk-seeking/taking person would be induced to take a certain payment if it is more than £50 (for example, £60) over taking the gamble.

Risk perception is a subjective judgment that people make about the characteristics and severity of a risk and this determines how they react to a risky situation. This subjective judgment means that people will arrive at different estimates and conclusions of how dangerous a risk is; so it is how they are conditioned and disposed of psychologically to such risky situations. Every time we cross a road or fly in a plane we are taking a risk. Although many millions of people fly each year, some never fly because they are risk averse. Some people gamble with money, others stay away from such activities; it is all a matter of personal choice and conditioning. Each individual will have a different perception of a particular risk situation and so will respond in a different way.

In the business situation risk aversion and risk taking also plays a part. Risk management involves making decisions about risks. If organizations refused to take risks they would not be able to take advantage of the many market opportunities presented to them. On the other hand, organizations cannot be governed by always taking risks on every aspect of their business. Furthermore, those individuals assessing and evaluating the risks and making the decisions may be risk averse or risk takers; it is always important, therefore, to remove any influence or bias towards risk taking or risk aversion. Ideally it is preferable not to work on a single opinion, assessment or evaluation of an individual but to work on the results coming from a team activity.

Of course, trust can play a key factor in influencing perceptions of risk. A business situation is perceived as more risky if the people, or organization, managing the business are perceived as untrustworthy, whereas if the business is being managed by trusted individuals then more credence will be given to this situation than from a management situation that is not trusted.

2.1.4 *Pure versus speculative risks*

Pure risks relate to loss but not to profit, whereas *speculative risks* relate to a profit or a loss. Most of the risks that businesses take tend to be speculative risks. For example, when the management reach a decision on a business venture or investment based on the chances of success, this could lead to a profit and commercial gain for the organization. On the other hand, the risk of the organization becoming infected with a computer virus, the theft of its commercial information or a denial of service attack represents a potential business loss for the organization. There are some cases where the boundary between the two types of risk is somewhat fuzzy and less straightforward – for example, which political or legal aspects are involved as is the case with data privacy/data protection legislation, legislation and regulations regarding telecommunications systems, or laws relating to forensic evidence.

Risk takers would normally fall into the category of those who are most likely to take speculative risks, unlike those who are risk averse. However, this does not rule out the risk averse being involved in speculative risks: it is a matter of management responsibility and the heuristics used by people to assess the severity and impact of the risk, whether by 'rules of thumb', educated guesses, intuitive judgments or simply common sense, and should not tend towards irrational risk taking or aversion.

2.1.5 Static versus dynamic risks

Those risks that are always present are referred to as *static* or *generic* risks and include, for example, floods, earthquakes, severe droughts and other natural perils. *Dynamic* risks are those that continue to evolve and change as society changes. They may be driven by economic or political events, new technological developments, social change, legal and regulatory changes and changes to the environment. Static risks are the same as pure risks, but dynamic risks could be speculative or pure. There are some categories of risk that relate to particular business applications, services or systems and so are not necessarily applicable to all organizations or to society at large.

There are some situations in which an organization has more control over the management of the risks, in particular those arising internally, and there are some risks over which the organization has very restricted management influence, such as external risks. An organization can do nothing to influence or control the risk of an earthquake happening, but it can minimize the damage the earthquake might have on its buildings by deploying certain technologies to strengthen the buildings and, therefore, control the extent of the damage.

2.2 Risk factors

There are many types of risk factor within the following categories:

1. Human resources

   a) employment protection

   b) skills and skill shortages

   c) employing people and the employment process

   d) operational deployment of staff

   e) internal versus external staff

2. Legislation, governance and regulation

   a) environment

   b) health and safety

   c) company laws

   d) employment laws

   e) criminal laws

f) data protection and privacy

g) intellectual property and copyright protection

3. Competition and business markets

a) pricing strategies

b) market positioning

c) speculating in new markets

4. Operations

a) business continuity and availability of resources

b) service level requirements

c) maintaining resilient and robust operational facilities

5. Finance and investments

a) returns and profit

b) long- and short-term plans

c) insurance

d) financial regulations

e) legal actions, penalties and liabilities

6. Security and safety

The risks relating to these factors can be rated according to:

1. Impact on business activities and operations

a) downtimes

b) drop in productivity

c) failure to deliver services or a drop in service levels

d) service outage

e) loss in performance

2. Impact on business strategy

a) failure to meet business targets

b) short-, medium- and long-term business effects

c) internal strengths and weaknesses

d) external threats and opportunities

3. Impact on owners/shareholders/company board/company image and reputation

   a) adverse publicity from business or operational failures

   b) drop in shares

   c) legal action

Given the range and diversity of risk factors, taking a formal and structured approach to risk management might be of limited value particularly if the organization does not do business in such a formal and structured way. This is especially the case if speculative risks are always being taken. It is vital, therefore, that any approach taken to implement an effective risk management process is not too rigid, but is as adaptable and flexible as possible to cover a broad strategic view of business risks.

2.3 Corporate risks

2.3.1 Corporate governance

According to the OECD's *Principles of Corporate Governance* [20], good corporate governance '... should provide proper incentives for the board and management to pursue objectives that are in the interests of the company and its shareholders and should facilitate effective monitoring'. While this directive clearly applies to large, publicly listed companies, it is obviously in the best interests of all businesses that their information risk should be assessed and managed. But, most importantly, effective business process monitoring depends on the effective measurement of information security risk.

While corporate governance can be seen to concern itself, in the main, with the assurance of the rights of shareholders and/or stakeholders within a public company, the corporate governance principles apply to any organization, particularly to those that form part of the supply chain for a public company, and especially if any part of their business is conducted online. The principles concerned are those of disclosure and transparency. An organization's ability to assure all business partners that its information is secured is part of supporting the governance principles of disclosure and transparency.

Specifically, the disclosure and transparency principles demand that information is prepared and disclosed in accordance with high quality standards and that channels for disclosure enable unimpeded, easy access to all appropriate information. Moreover, they demand that foreseeable risk factors are disclosed, implying an effectively implemented risk assessment process.

In summary, an organization's effectiveness, corporate governance, operational risk management and the legal and regulatory environment all serve as drivers for the implementation of an effective ISMS. The ISMS is as important to the operation of an organization as efficient and appropriate information and communications technology systems. Operational risks are risks arising from the execution of a company's business functions. It is a very broad area of risk and includes those relating to fraud, non-compliance with legislation as well as physical and environmental risks. The term 'operational risk' is frequently used in the finance sector, which must organize its risk management programme according to, for example, Basel II under which risk management is divided into credit and market risks, and operational risks. Credit and market risks are normally handled through an organization's financial department, whereas operational risk management is co-ordinated centrally and implemented in different operational units (so the IT department takes care of IT risks, the HR department takes care of personnel risks, and so on).

2.3.2 Information security governance

Information security governance is an essential component of corporate governance. It is a requirement of company directors to demonstrate due diligence in handling information assets on behalf of stakeholders. Information security governance includes all the processes and management decisions that affect company assets in terms of their confidentiality, integrity and availability for business. Without information security governance corporate governance policy cannot be met since there can be little or no assurance and confidence in the internal control system.

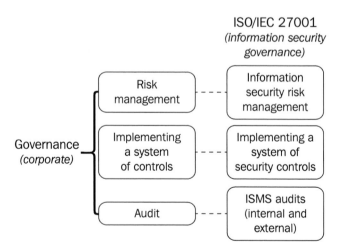

Information security governance encompasses all business assets, as well as their risks and threats, including information, processes, people, services, IT and reputation. Thus information security governance involves a risk management process, which includes IT risks, human resource risks, service risks, and so on. So, from the point of risk, information security governance has a greater scope than IT governance and its line of reporting is directly to the company board of directors and stakeholders.

The organization's policy regarding information security governance should recognize:

1. Information risks are an issue for the board of directors.

2. The accountability for information security risk management lies ultimately with the board of directors.

3. Information security risk management should support and achieve the organization's risk appetite and the approach to integrating risk in management decision-making, providing achievable goals for risk management. The approach taken should meet the needs of the core business activities.

4. Ownership and accountability for managing and reporting information security risks.

5. Roles and responsibilities for managing risk covering:

   a) direct responsibility for the management of risk – e.g. management and staff working within each organizational unit;

   b) responsibility for the development, implementation, maintenance and oversight of the effectiveness of the risk management framework – e.g. a risk committee;

   c) responsibility for providing independent assurance – e.g. internal audit; and

   d) ultimate responsibility for obtaining assurance and thereafter driving improvement. There is a need to take into account how people (e.g. staff) behave or are likely to behave within risk management processes.

6. A well defined and understood policy which sets out the requirements for managing risk and which is effectively communicated across the organization.

7. Well defined processes and procedures for information security risk management.

8. An effective method of assessing and monitoring the organization's information security risk management culture.

9. Clearly defined parameters around the level of information security risk that is acceptable to the organization, and thresholds which trigger escalation, review and approval by an authorized person or body.

10. A well defined approach to recognizing information security risk in management decision-making. Information security risks should be considered in decision-making when any significant business change is planned, be it acquisition of new IT applications, entering into a new area of business, or changing business processes.

11. Specific, timely, accurate and reliable methods of reporting, and an appropriate flow of risk information around the organization.

12. A commonly defined and agreed terminology for key information security risk management principles and practices.

2.4 Organizational risks

2.4.1 General

Organizations are exposed to various types of business risk, which can be categorized in a number of ways. One approach is to consider the source of the risk – examples being investment, legal, operational and market risks. Another is to consider the nature of the asset which is at risk – examples being people, property and information. A further approach is to consider the consequence of a risk in respect of its implications for the long-, medium- and short-term activities of the business – examples being strategic, tactical and operational risks.

An organization will also be exposed to a range of information security risks. These might be recognized as a major category of business risk in their own right or they could be subsumed into other categories, such as strategic and operational risks. An information security risk management system should be capable of dealing with all risks of this kind, irrespective of the way in which they are categorized in business terms.

Information security risk requires the effective control of processes, people and systems, and the monitoring of, and response to, external events. This Handbook aims to give guidance on assessing and managing levels of information security risk. Establishing, implementing and operating, monitoring and reviewing, and maintaining and improving the management system for information security risks is the subject of the related standard, ISO/IEC 27001:2005.

All organizations need to be aware of the need to manage information security risks. Viruses, distributed denial of service attacks, and the potential for system and network compromise could be seen as purely an IT issue. However, the ubiquitous nature of communications and information technologies means that the risks can sometimes turn out to be a complicated mesh of unmanageable interdependencies.

The OECD *Guidelines for the Security of Information Systems and Networks: Towards a Culture of Security* [19] states the need for '... much greater emphasis on security by governments, businesses, other organizations and individual users who develop, own, provide, manage, service, and use information systems and networks'. This greater emphasis is reflected in worldwide regulatory and legal instruments that place requirements on organizations to improve the management of the confidentiality, availability and integrity of their information throughout the business process. As a result, all businesses that use any form of information processing facilities, such as IT or the internet, have a significant role to play in the management of information security.

Organizations of any size have a number of processes, some of which are internally-facing and others externally-facing. In small organizations there will be limited resources to deal with this work so a number of these processes could be carried out by the same team or even the same person (see also the relationship between roles and responsibilities for organizational processes and assets described in Annex D). As information risk assessment is the responsibility of the whole organization, all parts of a business need to identify the information assets that are critical for their ability to function, and they should ensure that the related risks are assessed and the appropriate security controls are implemented and maintained to manage the identified risks. However, certain risks are specific to certain types of organizational process, and examples of these are described later in this chapter.

2.5 People risk

People-related risks are considered to be the greatest risk facing organizations today, and certainly in the future. These types of risk could be perpetrated by people using IT, deploying operational facilities and processes, or by those having specific organizational privileges and/or management responsibility. People risks can manifest themselves at all levels within the organization. People risks can be internal or external, or both.

Accidental risks might, for example, be caused by lack of appropriate training or awareness in the use of specific applications, services or systems. They are not motivated by personal gain but are the result of errors, mistakes or making bad judgments or decisions. On the other hand, intentional risks are driven by some motivation, for example, for personal gain, revenge, retribution for unfair dismissal, or the political reasons and views of social activists, terrorists or protestors.

The insider threat is of growing concern as the number of incidents in this area continues to rise. Staff can and do engage in a number of activities that could result in insider threat problems but the three main problem areas are IT sabotage, information theft and fraud.

Examples of fraud, which can be perpetrated by both insiders and outsiders, are:

- financial fraud;
- document fraud;
- identity fraud;
- computer fraud.

An organization needs to give its staff authorization to access and use its information systems in order for staff to do their work and to support the operations of the business. Depending on the type of authorization given, what privileges and access rights are attached to this authorization always leaves open the possibility that staff could exploit this authority to perpetrate harm or damage to the organization's information assets.

Many companies are facing problems with staff morale caused by such factors as downsizing and cost-cutting exercises, the streamlining of business processes, outsourcing of work, problems with the provisioning of staff pensions and many other issues. These problems, together with increases in stress levels, greater workloads and other staff pressures, are causing morale levels to fall which can open the organization up to a range of risks with disgruntled and de-motivated staff, and declining levels of confidence and trust in the organization. All of these issues can lead to some serious information security risks.

Another area relating to the insider threat aspect is that of the 'insider trader' risk. There are both legal and illegal insider trader activities. It is deemed to be illegal where a trader obtains non-public information during the performance of his or her duties within the organization, or otherwise in breach of a fiduciary duty or other relationship of trust and confidence, or where the non-public information was misappropriated from the company. A classic example might be the CEO of a company who learns, prior to a public announcement, that the company is to be taken over and so buys shares in the company knowing full well that the share prices are highly likely to increase in value. In this case the CEO has personally gained through his or her position in the company and access, at that time, to certain non-public information.

2.6 Operational risk

2.6.1 Risk within the scope of business operations

On the one hand, corporate and strategic risks are concerned with the organization's objectives and where it needs to go, how it plans to achieve these and the direction it needs to take, and how it can ensure its survival. On the other hand, operational risk is the loss of operations resulting from inadequate or failed internal processes, people and systems or from the effects of external events.

The operations of an organization are inextricably linked to the performance of its business and hence to its profit, productivity and ultimate survival in the market. Therefore, any risks to the operating environment and the subsequent impact can have a detrimental effect on business performance. The risks to the operational environment might be as a result of various changes: decreasing product life-cycles, the pace of innovation and the introduction of new technologies, obsolescence, changing economic conditions, commercial exploitation of the internet, staff shortages, lack of skilled staff or low staff morale. Many of the information security risks fall into the broader category of operational risk.

The rigid corporate boundaries that organizations once had are fast disappearing and in many cases their boundaries are more flexible, open, and in some cases almost non-existent. This is as a result of the changing business and economic conditions that have evolved. More organizations are dependent today on third parties as an integral part of their operations to achieve their business objectives and targets. This opening up of organizational boundaries has resulted in more risks being transferred across business and legal boundaries of different organizations and, with the widespread use of the internet, this transfer of risk can now be performed at broadband speeds.

The impact of this is that the organization needs to manage its operational risk outside of the confines of its old corporate boundary but to think in partnership with others to share and support the management of risk. It needs to adopt a flexible and more dynamic risk management approach; the staff and the organization's partners need to understand better how the risks will affect them and their operations, what their collective involvement needs to be and their part in managing the risks within the operational environment.

When a hacker gets into an organization's operational system, the hacker may subsequently be able to connect, using the networks of the organization, to the operational system of one or more of its business partners. This simple scenario can be expanded to detail other things that the hacker might be able to do having gained access resulting in some very serious security consequences. One immediate consideration is the legal consequences of the hacker having been able to obtain access to the third party operational system using the IT and networking resources of the organization to which the hacker originally gained access.

2.6.2 Externally-facing operational processes

Risks that are specific to particular externally-facing processes are as follows.

1. *Sales and marketing*
   These activities are a vital interface between an organization and the public. In any organization, there is potential risk from failure to protect the confidentiality of sensitive information during sales and marketing operations and of damaging the reputation of the organization through failure to ensure the accuracy and availability of information.

2. *Production and operations*
   Information used by the production and operations processes needs to be highly accurate and consistent, and available when required. The risks of failure should be clearly identified and addressed for those assets that are critical to the production and operations processes.

3. *Customer service*
   This process requires accurate information that is available when required. The consequences of failure are damage to the reputation of the organization, and consequent loss of business.

2.6.3 Internally-facing operational processes

Risks that are specific to particular internally-facing processes are as follows.

1. *Human resources*
   Information security risk is inherent in the interaction between employees and information systems. All employees therefore have a significant role in managing the risk position of the organization. This role must be addressed for recruitment, training, reward, discipline, to termination or change of employment.

2. *Research and development*
   These activities can result in significant risk if there is uncontrolled connectivity between the development and production/operations environments. Research and development can also create very sensitive information, such as that related to products under development. Those involved in such processes should therefore be aware of these risks, and of their responsibility for managing them.

3. *Administration and IT*

These processes are often regarded as having principal responsibility for the assessment and management of information security risk. However, it is essential that the interrelationship between information risk and organizational risk (see 2.4) is understood and, as a consequence, that information security risk assessment is undertaken by all functions and information security risks are not seen purely as an 'IT problem'.

4. *Finance and accounts*

Information security risk assessment is of primary importance to the financial and accounting processes of any organization. Good corporate governance (see 2.3.1) requires consistent and accurate financial information that can be traced from its point of origin to its point of use, through a transparent audit trail. The confidentiality of price-sensitive information, undisclosed financial results, and financial forecasts should also be maintained, consistent with business and regulatory requirements.

These are examples of specific information security risks in relation to organizational processes.

All organizational functions need to work together to address organizational risk through the development and use of an integrated and coherent strategy, as described in this Handbook.

2.6.4 Information security and operational risks

In summary, operational risks need to be considered to address the following:

- effects of information security on globalization;

- information security requirements of internal processes;

- information security requirements of processes interfacing with outsourcing and other third party services;

- information security in the deployment of human resources;

- implementation of information security in the use, application and management of IT;

- information security compliance requirements related to current and emerging legislation and regulation.

2.7 IT risk and IT governance

IT itself is not necessarily the security problem. More likely is how the IT is being managed and used. We can, of course, have examples of security problems that are purely IT-related, such as bugs or faults in software, lack of equipment maintenance, out-of-date upgrades, badly configured IT systems or hardware failures.

However the misuse or abuse of IT systems accounts for a far greater range of information security problems and this brings us back to a 'people' security problem, for example:

- lack of training can cause accidental misuse of IT, user errors and mistakes;
- deliberate use of IT for private use or for personal business, gain and profit;
- sabotage and destruction of IT;
- theft of IT;
- denying availability of resources causing a denial of service.

IT responsibilities as regards IT governance (see ISO/IEC 38500 *Corporate governance of information technology* for further details) include:

- becoming involved in business impact analysis activities with business units and managers;
- preparing proposals for and obtaining approval of risk treatment plans;*
- developing IT structures that implement IT control requirements;
- identifying and analysing threats and vulnerabilities within IT components;*
- keeping up to date with patches, etc;*
- implementing an incident response process;*
- conducting periodic reviews and audits;*
- ensuring that IT security is included during acquisition and development;*
- ensuring awareness regarding information security and user training.*

It is essential that the IT functions and management are in communication:

1. If IT is not in communication with management it will not be able to support business policy and objectives and will not be able to deliver the appropriate IT services and structure.

2. The IT department should understand the business objectives in order to put its IT services in the correct business context and to provide IT support that can protect the organization's information assets.*

The following are some of the expectations for delivery of IT support to the business:

- the IT capability is 'fit for the purpose' of meeting business requirements;
- a flexible IT strategy and structure to adapt to future requirements;

- able to meet business requirements with regard to throughput, response times, capacity, availability and performance;
- ease of use;
- robust and resilient;
- security of information and IT.*

*Note: * indicates that these objectives can be achieved by adopting ISO/IEC 27001:2005.*

There are several IT measures that may be used by a business to assess the success of its IT governance:

1. Increase in revenue

2. Return on IT investment

3. IT products:

   a) time to bring a new product to the market and sales from new products

   b) product quality

4. Services:

   a) level of service quality and delivery

   b) customer satisfaction

   c) delivery of IT value per customer/employee

5. Infrastructure availability

6. Cost of transactions

7. Partnering success

8. IT skills and competence

3 Risk Management Framework

3.1 Risk management

Risk management should be a practical subject. The theory of risk management is simple and straightforward to learn. However, applying effective risk management to practical problems is far more involved. As explained in Chapter 2, there are many aspects of an organization that need to be considered: organizational policy and objectives, operations, people, processes, IT, legal and regulatory, internal and external conditions relating to the business environment.

The organization should start by understanding what the vision of management is regarding information security risks, then to ask where is it now as regards this vision, where would it like to be, how does it get there and when will it know it has achieved that vision. The chapters that follow go through what needs to be done to be able to answer these questions.

What is the vision?	• Business strategy • Business requirements and objectives
Where are we now?	• Gap analysis • Risk assessment
Where do we want to be?	• Measurable targets of acceptable risks • Achieving an effective level of information security
How do we get there?	• Implement a system of risk controls • Have an improvement process in place
When do we know we are there?	• Monitoring and review process in place • Taking measurements

3.2 Information security risks in the organizational context

3.2.1 Business case

The implementation of an information security management system (ISMS) requires the deployment of sufficient resources. All organizations need to be clear about their reasons for implementing such a system. Different organizations will have different business drivers for undertaking the implementation of an ISMS. These drivers will derive from their regulatory or legal position, their status as a large or small business, whether they are a commercial, private, publicly funded or government organization, their geographical location, the type of business they are in, or the service they offer. The business case for implementing an ISMS should be clearly documented, and should set out the likely costs balanced against the benefits that can be derived from an increase in the ability to manage information risk.

The ISMS should not be established in isolation, but should take account of the organizational and operational risks and the overall business strategies in the organization. Annex C gives examples of the relationships between the different types of information security risk.

3.2.2 Scope of the ISMS

The scope of the ISMS should be defined in terms of the characteristics of the business, its location, assets and technology (see ISO/IEC 27001:2005, 4.2.1 a), and it should be well defined and complete, addressing the various elements mentioned in ISO/IEC 27001:2005.

Defining the scope of the ISMS is one of the most important decisions in the whole process, as the definition of the scope sets the scene for what will be involved in the ISMS. The definition of the scope of the ISMS is entirely up to the organization. The scope of an ISMS can be the whole organization, suitable part(s) of it, or merely a specific business process or information system.

The decision as to the scope of the ISMS should take account of the interfaces and dependencies that this ISMS has with other parts of the organization (that are not within the ISMS scope), other organizations, third party suppliers, or with any other entity outside the ISMS. An example is an ISMS that consists only of a particular business process. In this case, the other parts of the organization that the ISMS needs for its day-to-day functioning (e.g. human resources, finance, sales and marketing, facilities management) are interfaces and dependencies, in addition to all the other interfaces and dependencies that might exist.

The scope of the ISMS should be suitable and appropriate to the organization's capability and its responsibility to provide information security that meets the requirements determined by its risk assessment and by appropriate legal and regulatory controls. Indeed, such a scope is an absolute necessity for organizations seeking to claim conformity with ISO/IEC 27001:2005 (see 1.2 of ISO/IEC 27001:2005). It is important to note that, to claim this conformity, nothing should be excluded from the ISMS scope that might affect the organization's ability, and/or responsibility, to provide information security that meets the security requirements determined by the risk assessment and appropriate regulatory requirements.

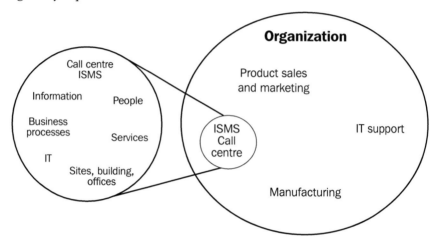

3.2.3 ISMS policy

Having determined the scope of its ISMS, an organization should then set out a clear and succinct information security policy to support the implementation of information security. ISO/IEC 27001:2007 states that the objective of the policy is: 'To provide management direction and support for information security'. The policy should be approved by management, and it should be ensured that all employees have received the policy and understand how it affects their work. This policy should be seen as a framework for setting objectives, giving management direction and action, and establishing the risk management context and criteria against which risks will be evaluated. Management direction and support is essential because the effective management of information security risk requires the deployment of significant resources, funds and management decisions to be made.

3.3 Risk management process and approach

3.3.1 Risk management process

The risk management process for ISO/IEC 27001:2005 follows the PDCA (Plan-Do-Check-Act) model as illustrated below:

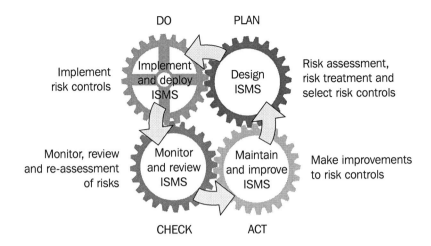

DO   PLAN

Implement risk controls — Implement and deploy ISMS / Design ISMS — Risk assessment, risk treatment and select risk controls

Monitor, review and re-assessment of risks — Monitor and review ISMS / Maintain and improve ISMS — Make improvements to risk controls

CHECK   ACT

Note that the generic PDCA model is used by other management system standards such as ISO 9001 (quality management system), ISO 14001 (environmental management system) and ISO 22000 (food safety management systems).

ISO 31000 (Risk Management – Principles and guidelines) is a generic standard and ISO/IEC 27001:2005 is an implementation of this generic standard focused on information security.

3.3.2 Risk approach

ISO/IEC 27001:2005, 4.2.1 c) requires the organization to identify and adopt a systematic method and approach to risk assessment. It is important that information security risk is managed clearly and consistently throughout an organization. However, managing the risks can employ different risk assessment and management approaches and various degrees of granularity that suit the organization's needs. It is entirely the decision of the organization as to which risk assessment approach is chosen. Whatever the organization decides on, it is important that the approach to risk management is suitable and appropriate to address all of the organization's requirements.

ISO/IEC 27001:2005, 4.2.1 c)–e) sets out the framework for the risk assessment approach to be chosen by describing the mandatory elements that the risk assessment process should contain. These mandatory elements are as follows:

1. Determination of the criteria for risk acceptance. This should describe the circumstances under which the organization is willing to accept the risks.

2. Identification of acceptable levels of risk. Whatever risk assessment approach is chosen, the levels of risk that the organization considers acceptable must be identified.

3. Identification and assessment of the risks. A number of mandatory elements need to be identified and processes carried out, described in more detail in Chapter 4 of this book. It is necessary that the risk assessment approach chosen addresses all of the concepts that are discussed in Chapter 4, as listed in 4.1.

4. Coverage of all aspects of the ISMS scope. The risk assessment approach chosen needs to cover all control areas in ISO/IEC 27001:2005, Annex A. The need for such comprehensive coverage is important, as several risk assessment approaches are in use that concentrate on IT only, and are not suitable for the type of assessment required by ISO/IEC 27001:2005.

The risk assessment should achieve a clear understanding of the risk-related factors that could affect systems and processes that are critical to the organization. Risk management activities should nonetheless be cost-effective and pragmatic. Effective risk management means balancing the expenditure of resources against the required degree of protection and ensuring that the resources expended are correlated with the potential loss and value of the assets protected (4.4 deals with the valuation of critical information assets).

The level of detail and complexity of the chosen approach has an influence on the effort and resources required during the risk assessment process. The risk assessment should be as detailed and complex as necessary to address all of the organization's requirements and what is required for the ISMS scope, but no more. Too much detail might lead to excess work, and a view that is pitched too high could lead to overlooking important risk aspects. ISO/IEC 27001:2005 does not require a highly technical or detailed approach, provided that all risks are appropriately addressed.

3.4 Risk measures

3.4.1 Risk parameters

In carrying out risk management there are a number of important parameters that must be considered:

- an assessment of the value of the assets under threat;
- the likelihood that a threat (or threats) will cause a risk of exposure to these assets;
- an assessment of the potential level of risk and the extent of impact in terms of damage, loss or harm;
- the threshold of acceptable risk;
- the level of residual risk.

3.4.2 Levels of risk acceptance

The organization needs to be clear as to the level of risk it is comfortable with. It should be clear as to:

1. Its criteria for risk acceptance. This should describe the circumstances under which the organization is willing to accept the risk.

2. Its acceptable levels of risk. Whatever risk assessment approach is chosen, the levels of risk that the organization considers acceptable need to be identified in advance of the risk assessment.

It is essential for the organization to define its criteria and levels of acceptable risk early in the risk management process. This is not something that can be carried out according to international standards; it needs to be performed in-house as each organization will have a different threshold of acceptable risk. Some organizations can cope with the risk of a £1 million loss but for other organizations this level of loss would be a business disaster. Other differences between organizations which will result in varying thresholds of risk acceptance and different criteria by which they accept different levels of risk are: capital resources, nature of business, current level of commercial well-being, future business plans, current business commitments, obligations and liabilities, and attitude to risk (i.e. whether they are risk averse or risk takers).

3.4.3 Residual risk

There is no such thing as a zero-risk situation. No matter how many controls or protective methods that are used to control risk there will always be a level of residual risk, which can never be reduced to zero. The residual risk is, therefore, the element of risk left over at the end of a process of implementing a system of information security controls.

Residual risk = combination of risk of exposure and control risk = combination of risk of exposure (likelihood of the threat being able to expose the system) and control risk (risk that a company's information security controls are insufficient to mitigate or prevent, detect or correct risks, errors or fraud)

The organization should consider whether the 'residual risk' is acceptable provided it can be demonstrated that all measures have been taken to limit the risk of exposure and the control risk, within the limits set by the organization in terms of costs and benefits.

3.5 Accountability and ownership

Ultimately it is the board that should be accountable to its shareholders for the actions it takes, the decisions it makes and policies it enforces regarding risk management, including the administration, governance and implementation of risk management activities. The directors are responsible for monitoring and reporting and are answerable for the consequences of its risk management activities, such as the adequacy of the system of information security controls. The board should assign appropriate roles and responsibilities to management to carry out risk management activities. In addition, the responsibility at board level for information security and risk management activities and actions should be clearly defined.

In turn, management have the responsibility to keep the board informed and briefed on information security risks, information security-related issues that arise, and the status of information security implementation and improvements. Management should engage information, systems and applications owners in the process as well as other interested parties and stakeholders.

3.6 Implementation of risk management

3.6.1 Delivering information security governance

Information security governance should be implemented to deliver the following:

1. Strategic alignment
   a) information security is driven by corporate and enterprise requirements;
   b) information security solutions should be fit and appropriate for business processes and applications;
   c) investment in information security should be aligned with corporate strategy and agreed risk profiles.

2. Business value
   a) complete information security solutions covering organizational, operational, process and technology;
   b) a culture of continuous improvement.

3. Risk management
   a) agreed risk profiles and criteria for risk acceptance/tolerance, as well as approved levels of residual risk;
   b) an understanding and awareness of the concept of risk exposure;
   c) an awareness of risk management priorities.

4. Performance management

3.6.2 *Risk management project and team*

Risk management should be implemented as a project. A risk team should be formed, with delegated responsibility from management for ensuring that the board's policy, strategy and risk objectives are being implemented, as well as requiring it to assess risks, propose risk treatments and information security controls, regularly review and monitor the risk profile of the organization, taking performance measurements and reports to the management on the status of the risk work. It is good practice to carry out risk management activities as a team effort and ensure that all interested parties (such as management, operational management, systems and application owners) are appropriately engaged in the risk management process.

3.6.3 *Awareness and competency*

Those who perform the information security risk assessments and other risk management activities should have:

- a basic understanding of how the business works and the organization's risk appetite;

- an understanding of the basic concepts of risk, e.g. how assessments of threat, vulnerability and impact merge to give a risk value;

- an understanding of IT to a sufficient level to enable IT threats and vulnerabilities to be understood, including a knowledge of hosts, workstations, storage devices, operating systems, applications, communication networks, websites, viruses, and worms, and how they work and inter-relate;

- an understanding of the different types of security control, how they work and any limitations – e.g. firewalls, intrusion detection systems, identification and authentication mechanisms, access controls, encryption, CCTV, logging and monitoring;

- a practical understanding of a suitable risk assessment method and any associated tools, software or forms;

- analytical abilities, i.e. the ability to isolate what is relevant;

- the ability to identify the people in the organization who will be able to provide the necessary information;

- sufficient interpersonal skills to obtain the necessary information from personnel in the organization and to communicate the results of the risk assessment in a way that is easily understood by decision-making management.

The risk assessor might be an information or IT professional, a security or information security professional, a member of staff from within the business, or an external security consultant.

3.6.4 Critical success factors

The following are some of the critical factors for achieving a successful risk management programme:

1. Management support and responsibilities

   a) establish an effective information security programme;

   b) the corporate security function reports to senior management and is responsible for executing the information security programme;

   c) policy enforcement is in place;

   d) the management endorse and are fully committed to information security, stressing the need for communication, awareness, understanding and compliance;

   e) senior management support to ensure staff perform their duties in an ethical and secure manner;

   f) engender an information security culture across the business;

   g) management lead by example.

2. Risk management

   a) management and staff have a common and adequate understanding of the importance of information security training, dealing with risks and threats, and they understand, accept and carry out their designated responsibilities;

   b) management participate in risk management activities at key decision points so that they 'own' the outcomes in that they were actively part of the process of developing them;

   c) there are clearly defined roles and responsibilities for risk management and management accountability;

   d) the levels of risk acceptance/tolerance and residual risks are clearly defined;

   e) responsibilities for defining, agreeing and funding risk management activities are in place;

   f) continue to make staff aware and vigilant of the threats and risks to the organization's information assets;

   g) implement risk management as a project;

   h) service level agreements are used to raise awareness and increase co-operation with suppliers;

i) proper attention is paid to risks related to data protection/privacy, copyright and other information security-related legislation.

3. Monitoring, reviews, audits and measurements

a) the information security function has the means and capability to administer information security to detect, record, evaluate, report, and respond to information security incidents when they occur through monitoring and measurement processes;

b) measurement processes are in place;

c) third-party assessment of information security policy and ISMS is conducted periodically;

d) critical infrastructure elements are identified and regularly monitored.

4. Keep things simple.

3.7 Risk management funding

The economics of risk is an important aspect of the overall risk management process. This is essentially concerned with providing funds to cover the financial effect of unexpected losses experienced by an organization. Without the right funding of the risk management process and management commitment to such funding, the organization will not be able to deal effectively with the risks it faces. It is sometimes difficult for an organization to calculate a return on its investment in information security, but the damage caused by the absence of efficient security controls can be far greater than the cost of implementing them.

The funding of information security is itself a risk associated with the balance between the business impact of higher funding costs as a result of implementing high levels of information security and/or the lack of availability of funding resulting in lower levels of information security.

There are many different aspects and options to risk management funding. The organization could include provision for residual information security risks in the internal cost of capital items, just as IT risks can be included in the cost of capital items for developing and running IT systems. The company, of course, could pay for the consequences of the effects of risk as and when they arise with no special financial provision beforehand. This could end up as the most expensive option depending on the loss and damage involved; for example a company with no business continuity process in place could, in the worse case, end up going out of business. The other end of the funding scale is to fund every possible risk scenario irrespective of the likelihood of the risk having an effect. The best option is a balanced management view on this, taking a middle way between the two extremes: spending just enough on information security, 'no more and no less', is sometimes easier said than done. During the risk treatment activity, the issue of cost–benefit analysis of risk management funding is dealt with (see 5.2 of this book for further information).

Some of the possible courses of action include the following:

- pre-loss, which involves the cost of prevention to reduce the likelihood of a risk of exposure;
- during loss, which involves the cost of protection to reduce the severity of the losses;
- post-loss, which involves the cost of recovery to reduce the severity of the losses and to make improvements to protect against future losses;
- paying for losses as and when they arise;
- internal contingency funds to meet the losses;
- post-loss loans to meet the losses;
- advanced contingency loans;
- use a form of risk transfer or sharing afforded by insurance.

Whichever approach the company takes regarding risk management funding, it is important that the funds are adequate to cover:

- the establishment and design of the ISMS;
- the implementation and deployment of the ISMS;
- the monitoring and review of the ISMS;
- continual improvement, maintenance and updating of the ISMS.

4 Risk Assessment

4.1 Assessment process

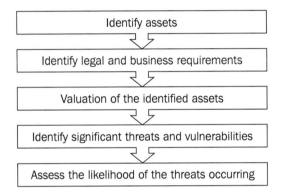

The assessment of information security risks includes risk analysis and risk evaluation, and depends upon the following factors used in these processes. The risk analysis should include:

a) identification of assets (ISO/IEC 27001:2005, 4.2.1 d), (see 4.2 below);

b) identification of legal and business requirements that are relevant for the identified assets (see 4.3 below);

c) valuation of the identified assets, taking account of the identified legal and business requirements and the impacts resulting from a loss of confidentiality, integrity and availability (see 4.4 below);

d) identification of significant threats to, and vulnerabilities of, the identified assets (ISO/IEC 27001:2005, 4.2.1 d) (see 4.5 below);

e) assessment of the likelihood of the threats and exploitation of the vulnerabilities to occur (ISO/IEC 27001:2005, 4.2.1 e) (see 4.6 below).

Risk evaluation should include:

f) analysis and evaluation of risks (ISO/IEC 27001:2005, 4.2.1 e), 3)) against a predefined risk scale (see 4.8 below).

4.2 Asset identification

4.2.1 Objective

To achieve and maintain appropriate protection of organizational assets it is important to have a clear understanding of which assets are included in the ISMS. Therefore, an inventory of all the important, and especially critical, assets should be produced and maintained.

4.2.2 Guidance

An asset is something that has value or utility for the organization, its business operations and its continuity. Assets need protection to ensure correct governance of the business and continuity of operations. The proper management and accountability of assets is vital, and should be a major responsibility of all management levels.

The important, critical and sensitive assets within the scope of the ISMS should be clearly identified and appropriately valued (see ISO/IEC 27001:2005, 4.2.1, and 4.3 of this book), and an inventory of these assets should be prepared, reviewed on a regular basis and updated and maintained as appropriate. In order to ensure that no asset is overlooked or forgotten, the scope of the ISMS considered should be defined in terms of the characteristics of the business, the organization, its location, assets and technology. Examples of assets and more information about asset identification can be found in Annex C, C.1. Grouping similar or related assets into manageable collections can help to reduce the effort necessary for the risk assessment process.

Governance and accountability for assets helps to ensure that adequate information security is implemented and maintained. An appropriate owner should be identified for each of the identified assets, or groups of assets, and the responsibility for the maintenance of appropriate security controls should be the assigned responsibility of the owner. Responsibility for implementing and management of security controls may be delegated, but overall accountability assets should remain with the nominated owner of the asset.

The asset owner should be responsible for defining the appropriate security classification and access rights for the asset, to agree and document these decisions and to maintain appropriate security controls. It is also the owner's responsibility to periodically review the access rights and the security classifications. In addition, it might be useful to define, document and implement rules for the acceptable use of assets, describing permitted and forbidden actions in the day-to-day use of the asset. Those persons using the assets should be aware of the rules relating to the correct use of the assets as part of their responsibilities.

4.3 Identification of legal and business requirements

4.3.1 Objective

To achieve and maintain appropriate protection of organizational assets it is also important to have a clear understanding of the business, legal, regulatory and contractual requirements that might need to be complied with regarding these assets.

4.3.2 Guidance

4.3.2.1 Sources of requirement

Information security requirements in any organization, large or small, are in effect derived from three main sources and should be documented in the ISMS:

1. The unique set of threats and vulnerabilities, which could lead to significant losses if they occur (these are considered in 4.5).

2. The legal, statutory and contractual requirements which are applicable to the organization, its trading partners, contractors and service providers.

   - ISO/IEC 27001:2005 defines two specific objectives with regard to assets: accountability for assets (Annex A.7.1) and information classification (Annex A.7.2).

   - The term 'owner' identifies an individual or entity that has approved management responsibility for controlling the production, development, maintenance, use and security of the assets.

3. The unique set of principles, objectives and requirements for information processing that an organization has developed to support its business operations and processes, and which apply to the organization's information systems.

Once these legal and business requirements have been identified, it is necessary to consider them in the asset valuation process (see 4.4) and formulate them in terms of requirements for confidentiality, integrity and availability.

4.3.2.2 Legal, regulatory and contractual requirements

The security requirements relating to the set of statutory, regulatory and contractual requirements that an organization, its trading partners, contractors and service providers have to satisfy should be documented in an ISMS. It is important – for example, for the control of proprietary software copying, safeguarding of organizational records, or data protection – that the ISMS supports these requirements, and it is vital that the implementation or absence of security controls in each of the information systems does not breach any statutory, legal or civil obligation, or commercial contract. Therefore, the legal statutory and contractual requirements relating to each of the assets and to the organization should be identified. Further information about legal and regulatory compliance is provided in Annex B.

4.3.2.3 Organizational principles, objectives and business requirements

The security requirements relating to the organization-wide principles, objectives and requirements for information processing to support its business operations should also be documented in an ISMS. It is important – for example, for competitive edge, cash flow and/or profitability – that the ISMS supports these requirements, and it is vital that the implementation or absence of security controls in each of the information systems does not impede efficient business operations. For each of the assets and the business activities within the organization, the related business objectives and requirements should be identified.

4.4 Asset valuation

4.4.1 Objective

To implement an appropriate level of protection for the organizational assets it is important to have a clear understanding of the value of the assets.

4.4.2 Guidance

4.4.2.1 Business requirements

Asset identification and valuation, based on the business needs of an organization, are major factors in risk assessment. In order to identify the appropriate protection for assets, it is necessary to assess their values in terms of their importance to the business or their potential values in different business opportunities. It is also important to take account of the identified legal and business requirements (see 4.3) and the impacts resulting from a loss of confidentiality, integrity and availability.

One way in which to express asset values is to consider the business impacts that unwanted incidents, such as disclosure, modification, non-availability and/or destruction, would have on the asset and the related business interests that would be directly or indirectly damaged by the occurrence of such incidents.

These incidents could, in turn, lead to loss of revenue or profit, market share, image and reputation, and these considerations should be reflected in the asset values.

4.4.2.2 Asset owners

The input for the valuation of assets should be provided specifically by the owners of the assets, who can speak authoritatively about the importance of the assets, particularly information, to the organization and its business, and how the assets are used to support the business processes and objectives. In order to consistently assess the asset values, a valuation scale for assets should be defined. More information about asset valuation scales can be found in 4.4.

For each asset, a value should be identified that expresses the potential business impact if the confidentiality, integrity, availability, or any other important property of the asset is damaged. An individual value should be identified for each of these properties as they are independent and can vary for each asset.

Information and other assets, as appropriate, should be classified in accordance with the identified asset value, legal or business requirements and criticality (ISO/IEC 27001:2005, Annex A.7.2).

Classification indicates the need, priorities and expected degree of protection when handling the information. It should be the responsibility of the asset owner (see also 4.2) to define the classification, as well as review it to ensure that the classification remains at the appropriate level.

4.4.2.3 Information classification scheme

ISO/IEC 27001:2005 requires that assets to be valued and protected according to the confidentiality, integrity and availability requirements of the organization.

Confidentiality

The following is an example for arriving at a confidentiality value for assets.

Value	Classification	Description
0	Public	Non-sensitive information and information processing facilities and system resources available to the public.
1	Restricted	Non-sensitive information but *restricted to internal use only*. This includes information that is not publicly available but is restricted information and information processing facilities and system resources available only within the organization based on business needs.
2	In confidence	Sensitive information and information processing facilities and system resources available on a *need-to-know* basis only, e.g. reflecting an organization's secret information. This would be a smaller group of users than the restricted group.
3	In strictest confidence	Sensitive information and information processing facilities and system resources available on a strict *need-to-know* basis only, e.g. reflecting an organization's top-secret information. This typically is an even more restricted group, i.e. a smaller group of users than the 'in confidence' group.

These classifications may have caveats appended to them to indicate a restriction based on a specific type of information such as:

- medical in confidence;

- personal in confidence;

- financial in confidence.

Typically 'financial in confidence' information might be restricted to those working in the finance department of an organization plus some senior management, such as the CEO and directors.

CASE STUDY

An organization has a public website to promote its activities, services and products. The information on this website would have an asset confidentiality value of 0 using the scheme above, whereas information relating to the organization's future acquisition plans would have a value of 3 and internal telephone numbers and other contact details might be given a value of 1.

Integrity

The following is an example for obtaining an integrity value for assets.

Value	Classification	Description
0	Low integrity/ criticality	The unauthorized damage or modification of information, systems and services is not critical to business applications and *business impact is negligible or minor*. This would cover cases where the criticality and/or accuracy of the information is a low or minor issue.
1	Medium integrity/ criticality	The unauthorized damage or modification of information, systems and services is not yet critical but is noticeable and would have an effect on business applications and the *impact is minor*. This would cover cases where the criticality and/or accuracy of the information is starting to be a major issue.
2	High integrity/ criticality	The unauthorized damage or modification of information, systems and services is critical to business applications and *the impact is of significant concern* to the organization. This would cover cases where the criticality and/or accuracy of the information is a major and serious concern.
3	Very high integrity/ criticality	The unauthorized damage or modification of information, systems and services is critical to business applications and *business impact is of the highest severity* and could lead to serious or total failure, disruption of business operations, processes, systems and application.

Typically a business working in the safety sector or supplying systems, services and products to this sector is likely to be working according to strict integrity requirements. Outside this sector there are many other applications requiring varying levels of integrity: the integrity of personal data, the integrity of the advertised service and product prices, financial data used in management decision making and information relating to online transactions and other e-business applications.

Availability

The following is an example for obtaining an availability value for assets.

Value	Classification	Description
0	Low availability	The asset (information, system resources/network services, people etc.) *can be tolerated to be not available for more than 5 days.*
1	Medium availability	The asset (information, system resources/network services, people etc.) *can be tolerated to be not available for at most 1–2 days.*
2	Medium–high availability	The asset (information, system resources/network services, people etc.) *cannot be tolerated to be not available for more than a few hours during normal working hours.*
3	High availability	The asset (information, system resources/network services, people etc.) *needs to be fully available during normal working hours.*
4	Very high availability	The asset (information, system resources/network services, people etc.) *needs to be available 24 x 7.*

Typically these are classification that may be seen as part of a SLA (service level agreement) that an organization has agreed with an external service provider or as part of an outsourcing arrangement.

CASE STUDY

An organization supplying managed data services to several businesses through various outsourcing arrangements is required to provide services that will provide a high integrity (value 3 in the above integrity scheme) and high availability (value 3 in the above availability scheme) processing capability by its customers.

4.4.2.4 From scheme to financial assets values

In practice, the asset and impact values are often required in financial terms. So, for example, an item of information may have a confidentiality value of 2 according to the classification scheme but senior management need to know how to relate this to the financial impact if this information is disclosed to one of its competitors. Therefore, the scheme tables above may have the descriptions extended to cover the asset value in financial terms. Hence a confidentiality value of 2 may relate to a financial value of somewhere in the range £100,000 to £250,000. This might represent the market value of this information as a market commodity if this information were to be leaked from the organization or stolen and then fell into the hands of other organizations.

CASE STUDY

Consider a simple system comprising a laptop and a range of information contained on the laptop. Let us assume this laptop is used by the managing director when at home and when meeting customers and clients on their premises.

The value of the laptop in monetary terms is easy to calculate. The value would be the purchase price of the laptop if it is new, and the replacement cost of the original laptop or the depreciation value if, say, one to two years old. For the purposes of this case study we can assume the current value of the laptop is around £800.

The information contained on the laptop is somewhat more difficult to calculate. In this case study if we assume the laptop contains confidential business reports, customer reports, financial data and personal data, the collection of information would have a relatively high value compared with that of the laptop. For the purposes of this case study we can assume the current value of the information is at least worth £100,000 in confidentiality terms to the organization that owns this information. Of course, it will also have an integrity and availability value. So, taken as a complete system, the laptop plus the information it contains, the overall value of this system as an asset is of much greater value than the value of the laptop without the information. Therefore, the overall value would be something in excess of £100,000.

If we scale this system up and take the same small organization with its internal IT and information systems, the overall value of the system is clearly higher. Let us assume the company has two servers, one for internal and external email and one used as a company database, plus 25 PCs networked together to have access to these two servers. The overall value of this complete system containing so much information is far greater than the managing director's laptop system. Clearly there will be far more information stored and processed in the system and so we can assume that the overall value of this information is going to be considerably higher than that on the laptop.

This case study illustrates that assets such as hardware and software assets taken on their own have a relatively small asset value compared with the information contained on this hardware and, when taken as a complete system of hardware, software and information, the overall value is at least as high as the value of the information the system contains.

4.5 Identification and assessment of threats and vulnerabilities

4.5.1 Objective

To identify those threats and vulnerabilities which, taken together, could compromise, damage or have a negative impact on the ISMS assets, it is important to have a clear understanding of which threats and vulnerabilities are involved to be able to assess the level of risk of exposure to the assets and, consequently, the level of risk faced by the organization.

4.5.2 Guidance

4.5.2.1 Identification of threats and vulnerabilities

Assets are subject to many kinds of threat. A threat can cause an unwanted incident, which could result in harm to the organization and its assets. This harm could occur from an attack on the organization's information, resulting in its unauthorized disclosure, modification, corruption, destruction and unavailability, or loss. Threats could originate from accidental or deliberate sources or events.

In general, a threat would need to exploit one or more vulnerabilities of the systems, applications or services used by the organization in order to successfully cause an incident resulting in damage or harm to assets. Threats may originate from within the organization as well as external to it. Examples of threats are given in C.3 and C.4.

Vulnerabilities are security weaknesses associated with an organization's assets. These weaknesses could be exploited by one or more threats causing unwanted incidents that might result in loss, damage or harm to these assets and the business of the organization.

The vulnerability in itself does not cause the harm; it is merely a condition or set of conditions that might allow a threat to exploit it and cause harm to the assets and the business they support. It is therefore necessary to understand the relationship between threats and vulnerabilities, i.e. which threat might exploit which of the vulnerabilities.

The key issue here is how likely is it that the threat will exploit a vulnerability? Therefore we need to talk about threats in terms of their likelihood of being able to exploit.

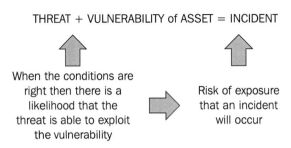

THREAT + VULNERABILITY of ASSET = INCIDENT

When the conditions are right then there is a likelihood that the threat is able to exploit the vulnerability

Risk of exposure that an incident will occur

The identification of vulnerability should identify the weaknesses relating to assets in the:

- physical environment;

- personnel, management and administration procedures and controls;

- business operations and supporting services;

- hardware, software or communications equipment and facilities.

Examples of vulnerabilities are given in C.5.

4.5.2.2 Existing implemented controls

Before starting either the risk assessment activities or the identification of threats and vulnerabilities, the already implemented security controls should be identified. This is necessary for a complete identification and realistic valuation of the threats and vulnerabilities, and is also important when considering the risk treatment options and what to do to manage the risks (see also Chapter 5). If this identification of already implemented controls has not yet taken place, it is recommended to do it prior to starting the threat/vulnerability assessment.

4.6 Assessment of the threats and vulnerabilities

4.6.1 Objective

To be able to calculate the level of exposure and risk the organization faces and subsequently implement an appropriate level of protection for the organizational assets, it is important to have a clear understanding of a likelihood value for each of the threats in relation to the level of weakness and vulnerabilities of the assets.

4.6.2 Guidance

4.6.2.1 Scales

After identifying the threats and vulnerabilities it is necessary to assess the likelihood that they will merge and cause a risk. This includes assessing the likelihood of threats occurring, and how easily vulnerabilities can be exploited by the threat. An example threat scale is illustrated below.

Value	Threat likelihood
1 (low)	Unlikely (e.g. less than 5%)
2	Possible (e.g. 5% – 29%)
3	Greater possibility (e.g. 30% – 49%)
4 (medium)	Likely (e.g. 50% – 69%)
5	Very likely (e.g. 70% – 90%)
6 (high)	Relative certainty (e.g. 90% – 99%)
7 (very high)	Certain (e.g. 99% and above)

The following table gives an example of a vulnerability scale:

Value	Vulnerability
1 (low)	Low of insignificant weakness – very high immunity from exploitation
2	Minor level or weakness and susceptibility to attack and compromise – high immunity from exploitation
3 (medium)	Serious but not major level of weakness and susceptibility to attack and compromise – medium immunity from exploitation
4	Serious and major level of weakness and significant susceptibility to attack and compromise – low immunity from exploitation
5 (high)	Extremely serious level of weakness and highly susceptible to attack and compromise – very low immunity from exploitation

4.6.2.2 Assessment factors

The assessment of the likelihood of threats should take account of the following:

1. *Deliberate threats*

   The likelihood of deliberate threats depends on the motivation, knowledge, capacity and resources available to possible attackers, and the attractiveness of assets to sophisticated attacks.

2. *Accidental threats*

The likelihood of accidental threats can be estimated using statistics and experience. The likelihood of these threats might also be related to the organization's proximity to sources of danger, such as major roads or rail routes, and factories dealing with dangerous material such as chemical materials or petroleum. In addition, the organization's geographical location will be relevant to the possibility of extreme weather conditions. The likelihood of human error (one of the most common accidental threats) and equipment malfunction should also be estimated.

3. *Past incidents*

That is, incidents that have taken place in the past, which illustrate problems in the current protective arrangements.

4. *New developments and trends*

This includes reports, news and trends obtained from the internet, news groups or other organizations that help to assess the threat situation.

Based on this assessment and based on the scale that has been chosen for the threat and vulnerability assessment (see 4.6.2.1), the likelihood of the occurrence of the threat(s) should be assessed. The overall likelihood of an incident occurring also depends on the vulnerability of the assets, i.e. how easily the vulnerability could be exploited. Vulnerabilities should also be rated using the appropriate vulnerability valuation scale (see 4.6.2.1).

Information used to support the assessment of threat and vulnerability likelihood is best obtained from those directly involved with the business processes at risk. It might also be useful to use lists of threats and vulnerabilities (see, for example, Annex C, C.3, C.4 and C.5) and links between threats and controls from ISO/IEC 27001:2005 given in Annex C.

4.6.2.3 Risk of exposure

The following table illustrates a simple way of calculating the risk of exposure (RoE) based on the use of a five-point threat and vulnerability scale where low = 1 and high = 5.

RoE = combination of threat and vulnerability (the likelihood that the threat is able to exploit the vulnerability)

Threat

Vulnerability		lo		med		hi
	lo	1	2	3	4	5
		2	3	4	5	6
	med	3	4	5	6	7
		4	5	6	7	8
	hi	5	6	7	8	9

Risk of exposure

The severity of the exposure is linked to the level of threat likelihood and the degree of weakness; therefore, the greater the likelihood and/or the greater the weakness, the higher the severity.

4.7 Impact value

4.7.1 Objective

To define expected damage, loss or harm value if the threat is successful in exploiting the vulnerabilities and causing a compromise to one or more assets.

4.7.2 Guidance

The question an organization should be asking itself is what would be the business impact if it could not have access to its business systems, applications and processes for one to two hours, 24 hours, three days, a week or a month? It is inevitable that the longer an organization is without its operational capability, the greater will be the impact in terms of business losses.

The impact value of the risk has a direct link with the asset values. The impact valuation can be linked to the asset valuation in different ways, though care should be taken to ensure that this is carried out consistently within an organization. Two examples are to:

- distinguish between risks for confidentiality, integrity and availability using the respective asset value as the impact value, thereby considering three different risks for each asset;

- combine the three asset values that have been assessed into one, e.g. by using the maximum or the sum of these three values.

Of course, there can be short-term impacts as well as long-term impacts. Take, for example, the case of the theft of a laptop containing commercial information. The short-term impact is based on the value of the laptop itself as well as the estimated value of the information stored on the laptop. However, there may be unforeseen aspects of this impact calculation that may only become apparent at some time in the future, such as the long-term damage to the organization's image or reputation, or the long-term loss in sales.

An information security impact analysis is likely to identify costs linked to:

- recovery from major system failures;

- loss of productivity;

- loss of services;

- loss of cash flow;

- loss of customer confidence, orders and sales;

- replacement of equipment;

- cost of resources to catch up with a backlog of work;

- loss of profits;

- legal penalties, fines, liability costs;

- damage to image, reputation and brand names.

> **CASE STUDY**
>
> An organization has a denial of service attack on its business systems. The immediate impact is the amount of downtime this has on the organization's operations with its systems made unavailable and inaccessible for almost 48 hours. This means a loss in productivity and/or delivery in services, loss of sales and revenue, failure to fulfil customer orders and/or service level agreements, and a loss of customer confidence. The financial impact of this attack will be a potential loss in profits. The customers may decide to change suppliers as a consequence. Depending on the nature of the contracts the organization might have with its customers there could be legal penalties for failure to meet contractual obligations and/or service level agreements.
>
> In building up its market position and rebuilding customer confidence the organization may spend three times as much on marketing as it normally does in the wake of this attack.

4.8 Risk calculation and evaluation

4.8.1 Objective

To calculate the levels of risk the organization faces based on the risk of exposure and the impact levels.

4.8.2 Guidance

The objective of the risk assessment is to identify and assess the risks, based on the results of 4.2 to 4.7. The risks are calculated from the combination of asset values expressing the likely impact resulting from a loss of confidentiality, integrity and/or availability, and the assessed likelihood of related threats and vulnerabilities to merge and cause an incident.

It is up to the organization to identify a method for risk assessment that is most suitable for its business and security requirements. The calculated levels of risk provide a means to rank the risks and to identify those risks that are most problematic for the organization.

There are different methods of relating the values assigned to the assets, the vulnerabilities and threats and to impacts to obtain assessments of risks. 4.4, 4.6 and 4.7 give examples of how risks might be calculated based on these factors. Common aspects of these different methods of calculating the risk are as follows.

A risk has two contributing factors: one expressing the impact if the risk occurs, the other expressing the likelihood that the risk might occur.

The likelihood factor of the risk is based on the threats and vulnerabilities, and the values that have been assessed for them. The threat and vulnerability values can be used in different ways, for example:

- adding or multiplying the threat and the vulnerability value and using the combined value;

- not combining the threat and vulnerability value and using them individually;

- when combining asset, threat or vulnerability values, care should be taken that no important information gets lost.

How the two contributing factors (the impact and the likelihood value) are combined to calculate the risk is up to the organization and the particular risk assessment method chosen. The only thing that needs to be ensured is that the risk level increases if any of these contributing factors increase.

A straightforward way of calculating the risk is illustrated in the table below with 1 being the lowest level of risk and 17 being the highest risk level. This table shows that increasing the risk of exposure and/or the impact level increases the risk level.

Risk of exposure

		1	2	3	4	5	6	7	8	9	
	1	1	2	3	4	5	6	7	8	9	
	2	2	3	4	5	6	7	8	9	10	
	3	3	4	5	6	7	8	9	10	11	
Impact	4	4	5	6	7	8	9	10	11	12	Risk levels
	5	5	6	7	8	9	10	11	12	13	
	6	6	7	8	9	10	11	12	13	14	
	7	7	8	9	10	11	12	13	14	15	
	8	8	9	10	11	12	13	14	15	16	
	9	9	10	11	12	13	14	15	16	17	

The organization may go a stage further and group the seventeen levels of risk as illustrated by the following diagram.

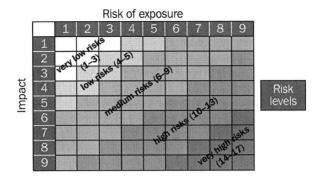

The next part of the risk evaluation is to compare the calculated levels of risk with the risk level scale that was defined when the risk assessment method was selected. The risk levels should be expressed, for example, in terms of loss for the business and recovery time, such as 'serious damage for the organization's business, from which the organization cannot recover in less than half a year'. Relating the risk levels to the organization's business is necessary to assess realistically the impact the calculated risks have on the organization's business and help to convey the meaning of the risk levels to management.

Risk level	Description
Very low risk (1–3)	The organization will accept these levels of risk since they have a *small or negligible impact* on the business.
Low risks (4–5)	The organization will accept these levels of risk since they have a *minor impact* on the business.
Medium risks (6–9)	The organization will accept these levels of risk since they could have a *very noticeable impact* on the business, which *needs to be monitored and/or dealt with as appropriate*.
High risks (10–13)	The organization will accept these levels of risk since they could have a *major and significant impact* on the business, which *needs attention as soon as possible*.
Very high risks (14–17)	The organization will accept these levels of risk since they could have a *very serious and critical impact* on the business, which *needs urgent and immediate attention*.

This risk evaluation should also identify the generally acceptable risk levels, i.e. those risk levels where the estimated damage is small enough for the organization to cope with in continuing their day-to-day business, and where further action is therefore not necessary. All other risks require further action and should be subject to the risk treatment and management decision-making discussed in Chapter 5. The results of the risk assessment process (i.e. the results of the processes described in 4.2 to 4.7) should be documented in a risk assessment report (see also ISO/IEC 27001:2005, 4.3.1).

5 Risk Treatment

5.1 Objective

Risks can be managed through a combination of prevention and detection controls, avoidance tactics and acceptance, or by transfer to another organization. This chapter discusses each of these approaches, together with useful decision-making processes for determining the appropriate approach to treating the risk.

5.2 Decision-making

5.2.1 Decision factors

Once a risk has been assessed, a business decision must be made as to how the risk is to be treated. Different business circumstances will dictate the kind of decision that is to be made. For example, a new technology-based start-up business might accept higher risks than a traditional, well-established organization.

The two main factors that might influence the decision are:

- the possible impact if the risk is realized, i.e. the cost each time it happens;

- how frequently it is expected to happen.

These will give an indication of the loss that might be expected to occur if nothing is done to mitigate the assessed risk. Information security risks can be difficult to quantify in terms of the probability of occurrence partly because of the lack of publicly available statistics on frequency of occurrence. The decision makers should therefore carefully judge the accuracy and reliability of the information upon which they are making a decision and the degree of loss that they are willing to accept.

In addition to considering estimated losses from security incidents, the organization will need to consider the cost of acting on the risk treatment decision – for example, the investment needed to implement an appropriate set of control objectives and controls as opposed to doing nothing, and the potential cost to the organization if something does go wrong. An organization needs to ensure that it achieves the right balance between achieving security and the benefits of protection, at the right investment, whilst staying profitable, successful, efficient and competitive.

Other factors that might also influence the risk management decision-making process are:

- the willingness to accept risks (also known as the 'risk tolerance' or 'appetite for risk');
- the ease of implementation of control;
- the resources available;
- the current business/technology priorities;
- organizational and management politics.

Considerations that are applicable to the role of information security and business decision-making are:

1. The principal role of those managing and treating information security risks is to convince colleagues across the business to deliver security through their everyday actions and decisions – not try to carry out information security for the company.

2. Those managing and treating information security risks are in the business of change management and continuous improvement rather than enforcement and work through the business culture and established trusted social networks.

3. Information security exists to help the company to protect its information assets as well as maximizing its investments and opportunities enabling it to take business risks rather than prevent them, and it should therefore be at the forefront of new business development.

4. Information security should constantly respond to new business concerns and, as such, the portfolio of responsibilities and their relative importance will change over time.

5. Those managing and treating information security risks and implementing security should never stand still or become fixed entities. Their role should be more concerned with overall corporate resilience than 'traditional' security.

6. Information security is both a strategic and operational activity, and those managing and treating information security risks and implementing security must distinguish between these two layers.

7. The power and legitimacy of those managing and treating information security risks and implementing information security does not come from their expert knowledge, but from their business acumen, people skills, management capability and their expertise to communicate effectively.

5.2.2 Costs and benefits

The loss of assets might be expressed in terms of the cost of replacing or reinstating the asset that is lost or damaged. This might indicate a need to spend money to protect against this loss, such as by implementing new, or improving existing, physical security if the asset happens to be a PC. It might be an information asset and so the cost of installing information security might be the cost of implementing new or improving existing controls, such as encryption and/or access mechanisms to avoid theft of information, back-ups to replace damaged information or digital signature techniques to check the integrity of the information.

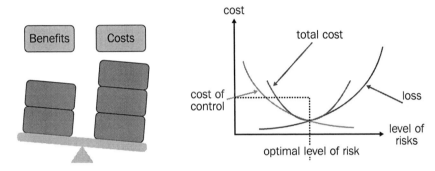

The loss of assets might be expressed in terms of the costs related to re-instating and maintaining the flow of revenue that the asset generates or provides.

CASE STUDY

An organization's website server is outsourced to a service provider. The organization uses this website to provide 24×7 online services to its customers. Over a period of time, the service being provided is starting to become unreliable and, on one occasion, it lost the availability of the website for 72 hours, which had a significant impact on its business, its revenue stream and its image.

The organization had no contingency plan to use a back-up server or supplier. Faced with this situation and the fact this could happen again, it needed to carry out a risk assessment and make a management decision as to the information security measures it needed to deploy to avoid this availability problem recurring in the future. The organization needed to weigh up the cost of these measures against the benefits gained or lost with or without these measures.

The loss of assets might be expressed in terms of loss or damage to the organization's image and reputation.

Cost–benefit analysis is a method that is used by some organizations during the decision-making process. This involves weighing the total expected costs against the total anticipated benefits of one or more actions in order to choose the best or most profitable option. Applying this in the field of information security leads to the following line of argument. What the organization needs to consider is the cost of implementing information security measures against the position of not implementing such measures, and assess these costs against the benefits to be gained or lost. Clearly if the cost of implementing the information security measures outweighs the value of the asset and the resulting impact of not implementing, then such measures would generally be considered not to be financially feasible. Of course, if the equation of cost-of-implementing against the value-of-the-asset were the other way round, then implementing the information security measures would be financially feasible. There is an exception to this in relation to legislation and regulation where the assets might take the form of a database containing personal data. Such data is protected by law in many countries, hence the organization is legally required to implement information security measures and failure to do so could result in fines and penalties.

It is the case that the accuracy of the outcome of a cost–benefit analysis is dependent on how accurately the costs and benefits have been estimated. If, in fact, the cost–benefit analysis results are inaccurate and are subsequently used in the management decision process, this may then lead to the introduction of risks caused by inefficient decisions having been made. The advice, therefore, is that cost–benefit analysis methods should be used with caution, observing closely the issue of accuracy of results.

Another cost issue is that of vanishing returns through overinvesting in security. Reducing the level of a risk by implementing a set of information security measures will result in a specific residual risk. If the organization decides to reduce the residual risk further by implementing additional information security measures, the cost of this will clearly increase. However, this process generally follows the law of diminishing returns which means that the more investment we make in implementing more and more information security measures does not provide the organization with an equally proportionate drop in residual risk. As the costs increase they will generally produce less and less reduction in residual risk.

Management methods other than cost–benefit analysis can also be used.

5.2.3 Return on investment (ROI)

In finance, rate of return (ROR) – also known as 'return on investment' (ROI), 'rate of profit' or sometimes just 'return' – is the ratio of gain or loss (realized or unrealized) on an investment relative to the amount of money invested.

$$ROI = \frac{\text{expected returns} - \text{cost of investment}}{\text{cost of investment}}$$

ROSI is return on security investment.

$$ROSI = \frac{(\text{exposure cost} \times \% \text{ mitigated risk}) - \text{solution cost}}{\text{solution cost}}$$

CASE STUDY – ROSI CALCULATION FOR A VIRUS SCANNER

A company has previously been infected with malware. It estimates that the average cost in damages and lost productivity caused by a malware infection is £25,000. Currently, the company receives four of these pieces of infected software per year. The company expects to catch at least three of four of these pieces of software per year by implementing a £25,000 malware scanner.

Exposure cost (i.e. annualized loss associated with a risk that has been assigned a quantitative measure before treatment with the proposed solution): £25,000 × 4 per year = £100,000
Risk mitigated: 75%
Solution cost: £25,000

ROSI = ((£100,000 × 75) – £25,000) ÷ £25,000 = 299%

But note this is the average cost in damages and a projected ROSI. If the four malware incidents each cost £5,000, £5,000, £5,000 and £85,000, the average is still £25,000. If a £5,000 piece of malware gets past the scanner, then the ROSI = 300%. If it is the £85,000 piece of malware that gets past, then the ROSI is negative.

A question that is often asked is: Is there any point in calculating the ROSI if the underlying data is inaccurate?

Past experience has shown that some industries have been successfully using inaccurate ROI metrics for decades and they have been able to obtain useful results, in particular when these results are repeatable and consistent. Therefore, if the ROSI method produces repeatable and consistent results, then ROSI can serve as a useful tool for comparing security solutions based on relative value. In the absence of accurate input into the ROSI, an organization needs to use consistent measurements for the ROSI factors that return comparably meaningful results. This approach has been put to the test in many businesses and has been shown to be much easier, and breaks through the barrier of accuracy that has kept ROSI in the domain of academic research. However, there is always room for improving the ROSI approach, which needs more research and development.

5.3 Treatment options

5.3.1 Reduce the risk

For those risks where the option to reduce the risk has been chosen, appropriate controls should be implemented to reduce the risks to the level that has been identified as acceptable, or at least as much as is feasible towards that level. In identifying the level of controls, it is important to consider the security requirements related to the risks (i.e. the threats and vulnerabilities, legal and business requirements), and all other results from the risk assessment. Controls can reduce the assessed risks in many different ways, for example, by:

- reducing the likelihood of the vulnerability being exploited;

- reducing the possible impact if the risk occurs by detecting unwanted events, reacting, and recovering from them.

Which of these methods (or a combination of them) an organization chooses to adopt to protect its assets is a business decision and depends on the business requirements, the environment and the circumstances in which the organization needs to operate. It is always important to match the controls to the specific needs of an organization, and to justify their selection.

There is no universal or common approach to the selection of control objectives and controls. The selection process is likely to involve a number of decision steps, consultation and discussion with different parts of the business and with a number of key individuals, as well as a wide-ranging analysis of business objectives. The selection process needs to produce an outcome that best suits the organization in terms of its business requirements for the protection of its assets and its investment, its culture and risk tolerance. It needs to be based on a clearly defined set of business goals and objectives, or a mission statement.

Controls to reduce the identified risks can be selected from ISO/IEC 27001:2005, Annex A, and also from additional sources, as and when necessary. This control set is the source that most organizations use. This control selection should be directly linked to the results of the risk assessment – for example, the results of the vulnerability and threat assessment might indicate where protection is needed, and the form it should take. Any such links to the risk assessment should be documented to justify the selection (or otherwise) of the controls.

Documenting the selected controls, together with the control objectives that they seek to achieve, in a statement of applicability is important in supporting certification and also enables the organization to track implementation of the controls and their continued effectiveness. Further guidance on the statement of applicability can be found in ISO/IEC 27001:2005, 4.

When selecting controls for implementation, a number of other factors should be considered; these include:

- ease of use of the control;

- the reliability and repeatability of the control (whether formally structured or ad hoc, and whether performed manually or programmed);

- the relative strength of the controls;

- the types of function performed (prevention, deterrence, detection, recovery, correction, monitoring, and awareness);

- the legality of the control, i.e. its compliance with the laws and regulations of the country/countries in which the control is being implemented – for example, the proposed control might include extensive monitoring of telecommunications or of traffic containing personal information, which could violate telecommunications or privacy laws.

5.3.2 Knowingly and objectively accept the risk

It is likely that some risks will exist for which either the organization cannot identify controls or for which the cost of implementing a control outweighs the potential loss as a result of the risk occurring. In these cases, a decision may be made to accept the risk and live with the consequences if the risk occurs. Organizations should document these decisions, so that management are aware of its risk position, and can knowingly accept the risk.

All key stakeholders should be made aware of, and agree to accept, the risk. When making a decision to accept a risk, it is therefore important that individuals with differing perspectives are consulted and as much reliable information as possible is gathered. Different perspectives might be obtained from individuals from other industries outside of the organization, or perhaps from within the organization from other functions or other geographical locations. Wider consultation can avoid possible bias in decision-making or group thinking where all the individuals within a decision group are blinded to specific facts or elements of the risk.

Where a risk is accepted as being the worst case, the consequences of the risk occurring should be evaluated and discussed with the key stakeholders to gain their acceptance. This could, for example, mean that a risk is deemed to be highly unlikely to occur but, if it occurred, the organization would not survive. When taking this type of risk, management might need to consult with key owners, shareholders, government agencies, suppliers and customers who might be affected in this worst-case scenario in order to gain their acceptance of the risk. Once again, the discussion process and outcome of these discussions should be documented so that any doubt over the decisions and the outcome can be clarified, and to ensure that responsibilities for accepting risks are clearly allocated. The outcome of such discussions may be documented in the statement of applicability.

Where such a risk is deemed to be unacceptable by key stakeholders, but too costly to mitigate through controls, the organization may decide to transfer the risk.

5.3.3 Transfer of the risk

Risk transfer is an option where it is difficult for the company to reduce or control a risk to an acceptable level or it can be more economically transferred to a third party. The term 'risk transfer' is also known in other contexts as 'sharing the risk' (as defined in ISO 31000).

There are several mechanisms for transferring risk to another organization. One example is through the use of insurance, where an indemnity is provided if the risk occurs that falls within the policy cover provided. Insurers, in consideration of a premium, can provide this cover after all the relevant underwriting information has been supplied.

However, even with insurance there is still an element of residual risk because conditions and exclusions will be applied depending upon the type of occurrence for which an indemnity is not provided. Transfer of risk by insurance needs to be analysed to identify how much of the actual risk is being transferred. Generally, insurance does not mitigate non-financial impacts and does not provide immediate mitigation in the event of an incident.

Another possibility is to use third parties or outsourcing partners to handle critical business assets or processes if they are suitably equipped to do so. In this case, care should be taken to ensure that all security requirements, control objectives and controls are included in associated contracts to ensure that sufficient security is in place. In addition, it is advisable to specify the security activities that should be undertaken in service levels, together with specific performance measures, so that activity and performance can be measured. What should be kept in mind is that residual risk is again present in that the ultimate responsibility for the security of the outsourced information and information processing facilities remains with the original organization, and that through the act of outsourcing new risks may be introduced, which will need to be assessed and managed by the organization undertaking the outsourcing.

5.3.4 Avoid the risk

Risk avoidance describes any action where the business activities or methods of conducting business are changed to avoid any risk occurring. For example, risk avoidance can be achieved by:

- avoiding certain business activities (e.g. not using e-commerce arrangements or not using the internet for specific business activities);

- moving assets away from an area of risk (e.g. not storing sensitive files in the organization's intranet or moving assets away from areas that without sufficient physical protection);

- deciding not to process particularly sensitive information (e.g. with third parties) if sufficient protection cannot be guaranteed.

Risk avoidance must be balanced against business and financial needs. For example, it might be unavoidable for an organization to use the internet or e-commerce because of business demands, despite concerns about hackers, or it might be not feasible from a business process point of view to move certain assets to a safer place. In such situations, one of the other options – risk transfer or risk reduction – should be considered.

5.3.5 Residual risk

After the risk treatment decision(s) have been implemented, there will always be risks remaining. It should be assessed how much the risk treatment decisions help to reduce the risk, and how much of a residual risk remains. This residual risk can be difficult to assess, but at least an estimate should be made to ensure that sufficient protection is achieved.

If the residual risk is unacceptable, a business decision needs to be made about how to resolve this situation. One option is to identify different risk treatment options, or more controls, insurance arrangements, etc. to finally reduce the risk to an acceptable level.

Whilst it is generally good practice not to tolerate unacceptable risks, it might not always be possible or financially feasible to reduce all risks to an acceptable level. In these circumstances, it might be necessary to accept the risk knowingly and objectively. The accepted residual risks should be documented and approved by management.

6 System of Risk Controls

6.1 Selection of risk controls

6.1.1 Objective

The objective at this stage of the risk management process is to select an appropriate system of information security controls that will reduce the levels of risk to the required levels of risk acceptance set by the organization.

6.1.2 Selection guidance

6.1.2.1 General

The selection of a system of controls should take account of the risk assessment results, the risk acceptance criteria, how much the controls reduce the risks, and the business, legal, regulatory and contractual requirements that have been identified.

Risk reduction is based on the selection of control objectives and controls to reduce the identified risks. Controls can be used to:

- reduce the likelihood of the threat occurring;

- reduce or remove the vulnerability;

- reduce the impact if the risk occurs, i.e. to reduce the impact from a security breach to an acceptable level;

- detect an unwanted information security event or incident;

- implement corrective action to recover from an unwanted information security event or incident and to stop the recurrence of the incident as well as correcting non-compliances with ISO/IEC 27001 requirements;

- implement preventive action against the occurrence of an information security event or incident.

In practice, a combination of controls is normally the way to achieve effective protection based on the uses indicated above. In addition, the controls that are implemented should complement and support each other. For example, technical controls should be supported by the use of procedural controls to make sure they are managed effectively.

ISO/IEC 27001:2005, Annex A, defines a set of control objectives and controls that can be used in the selection process. There are other control lists that also can be used to complement those specified in Annex A.

The control selection process should aim to achieve a level of protection that is commensurate with the risks to be reduced, and that the risks are reduced to an acceptable level to the organization in accordance with its risk criteria; this links back to the assets that are under threat.

6.1.2.2 Control objectives and controls

The control objective defines the goal of the security requirement, and a control (or controls) should be selected to achieve this goal. For example:

Risk prevention objective	Risk controls	Example threat/ vulnerability scenarios
To prevent user and system errors, losses, unauthorized modification or misuse of information in applications and processes	a) Data input to applications shall be validated to ensure that this data is correct and appropriate.	Lack of user awareness and training leading to user errors and mistakes. System errors or failures. Fraudulent activities. Insider misuse.
	b) Validation checks shall be incorporated into applications to detect any corruption of information through processing errors or deliberate acts.	System errors and failures. Software bugs. Lack of system maintenance.
	c) Requirements for ensuring authenticity and protecting message (data) integrity in applications, services and transactions shall be identified, and appropriate controls identified and implemented.	Information theft. Loss or corruption of information. Identity theft. Offline and online fraud. Unauthorized modification of information or software.
	d) Data output from an application shall be validated to ensure that the processing of stored information is correct and appropriate to the circumstances.	Lack of user awareness and training leading to user errors and mistakes. System errors or failures. Fraudulent activities. Insider misuse.

As is illustrated from the previous table the risk prevention and control objective covers a number of threat and vulnerability combinations and risk scenarios.

CASE STUDY

An organization decides to deploy a wireless network throughout its offices, which are located on two floors of a ten-storey high building in the centre of a busy town. In considering the risk prevention objectives, the organization has identified that unauthorized access to its network is one of the most worrying since it fears that unauthorized persons will then have access to some of its internal systems. Other objectives include preventing a range of risks that would follow if someone did gain unauthorized access.

In considering the objective of preventing unauthorized access, the organization will need to select a set of controls that would provide an effective solution to counter this risk. Wireless networks need to be configured in a way that will provide some level of protection, which means choosing appropriate control options such as using encryption either for WEP (wired equivalent privacy) or the strong encryption for WAP (wireless application protocol). Note WEP is a deprecated algorithm to secure IEEE 802.11 wireless networks.

In addition, the wireless system can be configured to protect the administrator password by turning off the Service Set Identifier (SSID) broadcasting and using media access control (MAC) address filtering instead.

As illustrated by this case study, a combination of controls are required to build a secure system of protection against the risk of unauthorized access. This combining of controls is typical for most risk scenarios.

In general, no one class of control is able to solve the organization's risk problems. Normally risk scenarios require controls that are a combined mixture of:

- management controls;
- legal controls;
- user controls;
- operational controls;
- supporting infrastructure and services controls;
- physical controls.

As an example, take the case of a piece of firewall technology or other security network technology. This type of technology is only as technically secure as it is securely managed and configured and kept secured.

6.1.2.3 ISO/IEC 27001:2005, Annex A

Annex A of ISO/IEC 27001:2005 provides a list of control objectives and controls that can be selected and implemented to reduce information security risks.

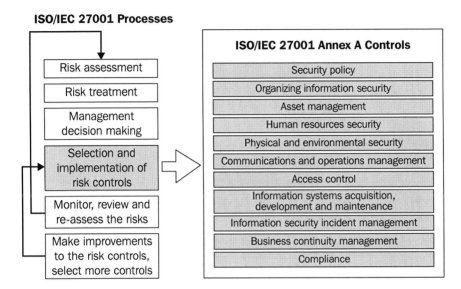

The following provides an overview of the 11 management control domains covered by Annex A. Each domain has one or more control objectives associated with it and for each control objective there are typically several controls defined which are collectively all, or in some cases singularly, designed to meet the requirements of the objective.

Annex A management control domains	General scope
Security policy	Policy giving the security mission and objectives of the organization
Organization of information security	Procedures, measures and process relating to how the organization structures, forms and co-ordinates its staff and related resources to achieve efficient and effective management of its security activities
Asset management	Procedures and process relating to achieving effective management of organizational assets to ensure that appropriate protection is given to the different types/class and values of asset

Annex A management control domains	General scope
Human resources security	Policy, procedures, technical measures and process relating to all the phases of staff employment from recruitment and deployment to termination
Physical and environmental security	Physical measures for protecting organizational buildings, offices, equipment, hardware and cabling
Communications and operations security	Policy and procedures for the protecting the deployment, use and management of communications and operational facilities of the organization
Access controls	Policy, procedures, technical measures and process relating to all forms of access control deployment, use and management covering access to information, applications, services and operating system
Information systems acquisition, development and maintenance	Policy, procedures and process relating to the acquisition, development and maintenance of information systems to ensure effective protection of organizational assets.
Information security incident management	Procedures and process relating to deployment, use and management of an information security incident programme.
Business continuity management	Plans, procedures and process relating to the information security aspects of business continuity.
Compliance	Procedures, measures and process relating to the compliance with legal, regulatory and contractual requirements, commitments and obligations.

The scope of Annex A covers information security at different levels: people, information itself, organizational, operational, processes and applications, services, legal and physical. Hence a system of controls based on these 11 domains gives a good framework to provide a holistic management system approach to protecting the organization's assets.

The control objectives are in most cases worded in terms of requirements as per an underlying threat, vulnerability or risk, as illustrated in the example given in 6.1.2.2.

The following is an example of one of the objectives in Annex A, which is worded generically to reflect the range of asset groups, threats, vulnerabilities or risks that the objective is aimed at preventing:

Objective	Asset group	Example list of threats	Example list of vulnerabilities	Example list of controls based on Annex A
To prevent unauthorized access	Information	• Hacking • Unauthorized insider access • Social engineering • Espionage	• Weak or no access control methods • Weak or no identification and authentication methods • Software weaknesses • Lack of, or ineffective, policies • Lack of, or ineffective, procedures • Lack of user awareness and training • Lack of roles and responsibilities • Lack of software controls	• Information handling procedures • Information classification guidelines • Acceptable use policy • Change management • Segregation of duties • Separation of development, testing and operational facilities • Controls protecting networks and services • Controls for the management of removable media • Secure disposal of information on media • Controls securing system documentation • Information exchange policies, procedures and agreements • Controls for secure e-commerce online transactions • Controls for monitoring unauthorized activities
	Applications			
	Network services			
	Operating and system software			

Objective	Asset group	Example list of threats	Example list of vulnerabilities	Example list of controls based on Annex A
	Information (*continued*)			• Protection of audit logs • Access control policy • Controls for user access management • User responsibilities • Controls for protecting access to networks
	Applications (*continued*)			• Authentication controls • Controls for securing remote access • Controls on the use of system utilities • Information access restriction • Sensitive system isolation
	Network services (*continued*)			• Control of operational software • Protection of system test data • Access control to program source code • Controls regarding operating system changes
	Operating and system software (*continued*)			• Restrictions on changes to software packages • Managing and control of technical vulnerabilities • Incident handling procedures

Objective	Asset group	Example list of threats	Example list of vulnerabilities	Example list of controls based on Annex A
	Physical assets	• Breaking and entry into buildings and offices • Social engineers • Unaccompanied visitors, contractors or maintenance staff • Theft of equipment and media	• Little or no physical control of buildings, offices, server rooms, research and development labs • No physical protection of equipment, media or cabling	• Physical security perimeter • Physical entry controls • Securing offices, rooms and facilities • Protecting against external and environmental threats • Working in secure areas • Public access, delivery and loading areas • Equipment siting and protection • Cabling security • Correct equipment maintenance • Secure use of equipment off site • Secure disposal or re-use of equipment • Authorized removal of property • Protecting physical media in transit

The controls in this table associated with the objective of preventing unauthorized access are aimed at countering these example threats and/or overcoming these example vulnerabilities. Not all of these controls may need to be implemented. The controls that need to be considered for implementation will, of course, depend on the risk assessment results and the risks that need to be reduced in accordance with the organization's particular criteria on risk acceptance.

CASE STUDY

A company's networked database server

A company's database server provides access to all its 200 employees. It is connected to the internet via firewall on the external perimeter of the organization's network system. The server is connected to three other servers within the company, one of which has restricted access to 20 researchers. The other two servers have restricted access to those in the finance department and to senior management.

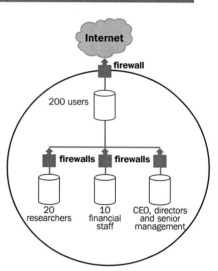

Examples of the threats and risks faced by the company:

CAUSES	Information security incidents	EFFECTS
Misuse of system resources Abuse of privileges and access rights Lack of access control or weak access control Phishing attack Social engineering attack	Theft of information	Financial impact Failure to deliver services Non-compliance with privacy laws Impact on business image

CAUSES
(threats, vulnerabilities)

Potential
information
security incidents

EFFECTS

Financial impact
Failure to deliver products
System crashes
System performance loss
Loss of confidential
information
Loss of productivity
Failure to meet contracts
Loss of business in the
market

DDoS attacks
Spam warfare attack
Virus, worm or Trojan
Horse attack

Disruption or denial
of services

CAUSES
(threats, vulnerabilities)

Potential
information
security incidents

EFFECTS

Lack of maintenance
Lack of system testing
Lack of software updates
and patches
High demand for system
availability beyond its
running capacity

System failure

Disruption to operations
System downtime and
impact on delivery of
services leading to loss of
business and customer
confidence
Denial of access to
information systems

The risks the company faces related to these areas of threat are
indicated below:

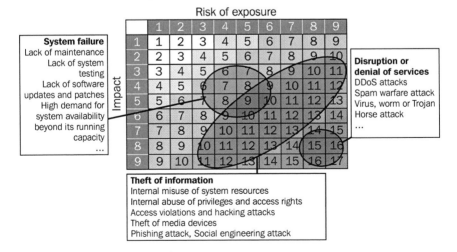

Risk of exposure

System failure
Lack of maintenance
Lack of system
testing
Lack of software
updates and patches
High demand for
system availability
beyond its running
capacity
...

**Disruption or
denial of services**
DDoS attacks
Spam warfare attack
Virus, worm or Trojan
Horse attack
...

Theft of information
Internal misuse of system resources
Internal abuse of privileges and access rights
Access violations and hacking attacks
Theft of media devices
Phishing attack, Social engineering attack

	information handling procedures (7.2.2)
	physically secure areas (9.1)
	equipment security (9.2)
Some of the	operating procedures (10.1.1)
contents from	protection against malicious code (10.4)
ISO/IEC 27001	back-ups (10.5)
Annex A that	network security management (10.6)
could help	access control policy (11.1.1)
in reducing	user access (11.2–11.3)
the identified	network access (11.4)
security risks	application and information access control (11.6)
	authentication and identification controls (11.2–11.5)
	security of system files (12.4.1–12.4.3)
	vulnerability and patch management (12.6)

6.1.2.4 Grouping controls

Each of the Annex A control domains covers one or more different types of asset group as illustrated in the table below.

Annex A management control domains	Asset groups
Security policy	All organization assets
Organization of information security	People, information and service assets
Asset management	All organization assets
Human resources security	People and information assets
Physical and environmental security	Physical assets (buildings, offices, equipment, hardware, cabling)
Communications and operations security	All organization assets
Access controls	Information, applications, services and operating system assets
Information systems acquisition, development and maintenance	Systems, processes and software assets
Information security incident management	All organization assets
Business continuity management	All organization assets
Compliance	All organization assets

Management control domains	Management and legal	Users	Operational	Support (e.g. IT services, external services)	Physical security
Security policy	Management direction and commitment				
Organization of information security	Roles and responsibilities Co-ordination activities and management review meetings				
Asset management	Inventories, asset ownership Information classification, acceptable use				
Human resources security					
Physical and environmental security	Off-site use of equipment Equipment disposal	Off-site use of equipment Equipment disposal	Equipment maintenance Off-site use of equipment	Equipment maintenance Off-site use of equipment	Physical access Equipment maintenance
Communications and operations security	Policies and procedures	Policies and procedures Malware and malicious code protection	Policies and procedures Malware and malicious code protection	Policies and procedures Malware and malicious code protection	Policies and procedures
Access controls	Policies and procedures	Policies and procedures Information Network services Applications	Policies and procedures Information Network services Applications	Policies and procedures Information Network services Operating systems Applications Monitoring access System software and utilities management	

Management control domains	Management and legal	Users	Operational	Support (e.g. IT services, external services)	Physical security
Information systems acquisition, development and maintenance	Cryptographic policy	Correct information processing Use of cryptography	Correct information processing Use of cryptography Protection of system files	Integration of security in systems Protection of system files Software maintenance Software development Vulnerability management (e.g. patches)	
Information security incident management	Reporting Incident response activities	Reporting Incident response activities	Procedures Incident response activities	Procedures Incident response activities Incident handling team	Incident response activities
Business continuity management	Plans and procedures Review of plans	Procedures	Procedures Testing plans Review of plans	IT readiness for business continuity Testing plans	Procedures Testing plans
Compliance	Legal advice Implement legal, regulatory or contractual requirements	Implement legal, regulatory or contractual requirements			

6.2 Implementation of risk controls

6.2.1 Objective

The objective at this stage of the risk management process is to implement the selected system of information security controls.

6.2.2 Implementation guidance

6.2.2.1 General

Annex A of ISO/IEC 27001 provides a list of controls that can be selected and implemented. In addition, ISO/IEC 27002 provides implementation guidance for each of these controls. It is not mandatory to follow this guidance, although it is best practice guidance that has been used by a very large number of organizations for at least the last 20 years. Such guidance has therefore been used, tested and re-tested many times. Although the guidance in ISO/IEC 27002 is practical as well as being generic, it should not be viewed as the definitive advice on how to implement the controls and an organization may need to seek additional guidance and/or customize the guidance to its particular information security needs.

6.2.2.2 Policies and procedures

Annex A covers high-level as well as more detailed policies and procedures across all of the control domains shown in the table in 6.1.2.3. The information security policy specified in ISO/IEC 27001 Annex A.5.1 is the overriding management policy, with which all other policies, procedures, plans, instruction manuals and organization security codes must comply. These supporting policies and procedures should provide the rules and instructions to be followed to implement the high-level information security policy. The diagram below illustrates some of these policies and procedures from Annex A, placed in a hierarchical order.

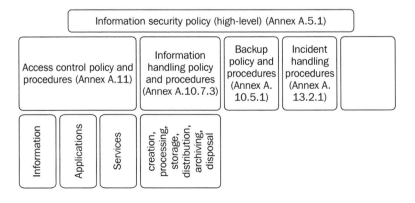

The following are good practices regarding the implementation of policies and procedures:

- Management commitment shall make sure the policies and procedures are approved, distributed and used.

- Policies and procedures are regularly reviewed and updated.

- Policies and procedures should be written in a clear, concise and user-friendly way.

- Management shall provide training and awareness in the use of policies and procedures.

- An electronic documentation system for policies and procedures using an internal networking system should be considered as this makes their distribution and use much easier.

- The correct versions shall always be used.

6.2.3 Incident handling process, disaster recovery and business continuity

6.2.3.1 General

The importance of having an effective incident handling process in place cannot be emphasized enough. The same applies to the importance of business continuity and disaster recovery: plans must be in place, they need to be tested and exercised, and reviewed and updated on a regular basis. The incident handling process should be seen as a management tool for not only detecting, assessing and resolving incidents but also as a useful security measure. The question is: 'Is the organization to spend most of its time resolving serious incidents of yesterday, or is it to be more proactive and stay ahead of the game by resolving minor incidents and protecting future business continuity?'

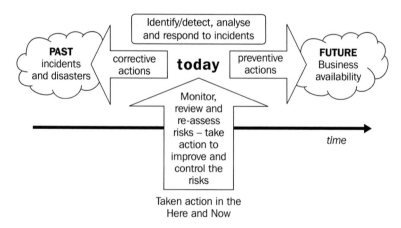

When a serious incident occurs, normal levels of operations can be disrupted, possibly leaving the organization without the capability to conduct any business – a complete shutdown of its operations. One important consideration is the period of disruption and outage that the organization can tolerate. How much data is it willing to lose in the event of a disaster? How much downtime is tolerable?

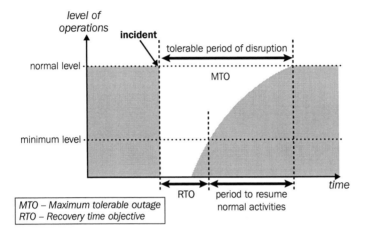

Both the recovery point objective (RPO) and recovery time objective (RTO) should be determined by undertaking a business impact analysis. An example of the RPO is the recovery of data to a previous point in time, and RTO is relevant to how much downtime the business is willing to tolerate.

A further consideration involves the time needed to catch up with processing data that arrived during the downtime but has not been processed. For example, an organization may use a call centre to manually record information for future processing, and an upstream system not affected by a disaster may continue to produce and store data while a downstream system is not available.

CASE STUDY

If the RPO of a company is two hours and the time it takes to get the data back into production is five hours, the RPO is still two hours. Based on this RPO, the data must be restored to within two hours of the disaster.

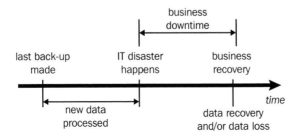

EXAMPLE

If there is a complete replication at 10.00 a.m. and the system dies at 11.59 a.m. without a new replication, the loss of the data written between 10.00 a.m. and 11.59 a.m. will not be recovered from the replica. This amount of time during which data has been lost has been deemed acceptable because of the two-hour RPO. This is the case even if it takes an additional three hours to get the site back into production. The production will continue from the point in time of 10.00 a.m. All data in between will have to be manually recovered through other means.

6.2.3.2 Incident handling process

The following shows the main stages of the incident handling process:

ISO/IEC 27001 ANNEX A.13

A.13.1 Reporting information security events and weaknesses

Objective: To ensure that information security events and weaknesses associated with information systems are communicated in a manner that allows timely corrective action to be taken.

Reporting information security events
Information security events shall be reported through appropriate management channels as quickly as possible.

Reporting security weaknesses
All employees, contractors and third party users of information systems and services shall be required to note and report any observed or suspected security weaknesses in systems or services.

A.13.2 Management of information security incidents and improvements

Objective: To ensure that a consistent and effective approach is applied to the management of information security incidents.

Responsibilities and procedures
Management responsibilities and procedures shall be established to ensure a quick, effective, and orderly response to information security incidents.

Learning from information security incidents
There shall be mechanisms in place to enable the types, volumes, and costs of information security incidents to be quantified and monitored.

Collection of evidence
Where, after an information security incident, a follow-up action against
a person or organization involves legal action (either civil or criminal),
evidence shall be collected, retained, and presented to conform to the
rules of evidence laid down in the relevant jurisdiction(s).

6.2.3.3 Business continuity

ISO/IEC 27001 ANNEX **A.14,** BUSINESS CONTINUITY MANAGEMENT

Information security aspects of business continuity management

Objective: To counteract interruptions to business activities, to protect
critical business processes from the effects of major failures of
information systems or disasters, and to ensure their timely resumption.

*Include information security in the business continuity
management process*
A managed process shall be developed and maintained for business
continuity throughout the organization that addresses the information
security requirements needed for the organization's business continuity.

Business continuity and risk assessment
Events that can cause interruptions to business processes shall be
identified, along with the probability and impact of such interruptions
and their consequences for information security.

*Developing and implementing continuity plans, including
information security*
Plans shall be developed and implemented to maintain or restore
operations and ensure the availability of information at the required
level and in the required time scales following interruption to, or failure
of, critical business processes.

Business continuity planning framework
A single framework of business continuity plans shall be maintained
to ensure that all plans are consistent, to address information security
requirements consistently, and to identify priorities for testing and
maintenance.

Testing, maintaining and reassessing business continuity plans
Business continuity plans shall be tested and updated regularly to
ensure that they are up to date and effective.

6.2.4 Technical controls

ISO/IEC 27001 is a management standard and all the controls are used to manage the risks faced by the organization. Some of the controls are policies and procedures used by all employees. Others are more technical in nature and apply to a smaller group of employees that have been assigned specific information security tasks, for example, controls used for the management of network services, access control methods, identification and authentication techniques, and software. The following provides some examples.

ISO/IEC 27001 ANNEX

A.11.4 Network access control

Objective: To prevent unauthorized access to networked services.

User authentication for external connections
Appropriate authentication methods shall be used to control access by remote users.

Remote diagnostic and configuration port protection
Physical and logical access to diagnostic and configuration ports shall be controlled.

Segregation in networks
Groups of information services, users, and information systems shall be segregated on networks.

Network connection control
For shared networks, especially those extending across the organization's boundaries, the ability of users to connect to the network shall be restricted, in line with the access control policy and requirements of the business applications.

A.12.5 Security in development and support processes

Objective: To maintain the security of application system software and information.

Technical review of applications after operating system changes
When operating systems are changed, business critical applications shall be reviewed and tested to ensure there is no adverse impact on organizational operations or security.

A.12.6 Technical vulnerability management

Objective: To reduce risks resulting from the exploitation of published technical vulnerabilities.

Control of technical vulnerabilities
Timely information about technical vulnerabilities of information
systems being used shall be obtained, the organization's exposure
to such vulnerabilities evaluated, and appropriate measures taken to
address the associated risk.

6.2.5 Training and awareness

6.2.5.1 General

It is important that a company ensures that all personnel who are assigned
information security responsibilities are competent to perform the required
information security tasks. The company therefore should provide the necessary
training and awareness to those staff that are involved in:

- establishing, implementing, operating, monitoring, reviewing, maintaining and
  improving an ISMS;

- carrying out risk assessments;

- the incident response team;

- IT security;

- physical security;

- carrying out security audits and reviews.

In addition, an organization needs to provide general training and awareness to all
staff regarding:

- the risks that the organization faces with regard to its day-to-day tasks (see risk
  management culture, 6.2.5.2);

- use of the company's information security policies and procedures;

- complying with legal and regulatory requirements and contractual security
  obligations relevant to the information security management.

6.2.5.2 Risk management culture

An important aspect of risk control is to engender a risk management culture
within the organization to ensure that management and employee thinking,
attitudes, behaviour, processes and practices towards risk at all levels become an
integral daily part of the way in which the organization operates.

Developing a risk management culture is a critical part of the risk management
process. It is also one of the most difficult aspects to achieve as building a

cultural awareness with the necessary management and employee competence, knowledge and capability takes time. In addition, business attitudes change and the organization faces a changing mind set and behaviour within its workforce.

The organization should define its risk culture, and consider what different stakeholder groups need from risk management.

Risk management culture should be established as a collective effort by stakeholders across the organization. A risk management culture will, of course, depend on the nature, scale and complexity of the organization; it should, however, exhibit the following features:

- clear evidence of support from the top management of the organization;

- a clear understanding of the role of risk and the benefits of risk management throughout the organization;

- all staff have an awareness of risk management, their roles and responsibilities, and sufficient risk management skills, knowledge and competence in line with the risk role/risk element of any role they are required to perform on a daily basis;

- risk management is an automatic aspect of working practices – staff should consider risk without being prompted;

- open and honest discussion around risk;

- risk information is shared across the company and lessons learned from actual incidents;

- risk management is part of company performance.

6.2.5.3 Awareness programme

An awareness programme should begin with the support of senior management. Ideally the CEO should launch the programme by, for example, sending an email message, which briefly summarizes the risks and threats and states that security is the responsibility of everyone in the company. It is also a good idea to incorporate relevant information security content into other training programmes, for example, staff induction and training on how to do a particular job.

Distribute security awareness tips by email on a regular basis to advise best practices and reinforce policy. Here are a few topics to start off with:

- viruses and other malicious software;

- passwords;

- workstation, PC and laptop security;

- business continuity;

- destruction of sensitive material;

- taking photographs;

- use of mobile devices;

- social engineering and not being afraid to say 'no';

- operational security;

- backing up data;

- security incidents.

Additional awareness methods include arranging security lunches and seminars, a security website and awareness posters. The awareness site should have a security representative to assist in the awareness programme and address security incidents. An 'information security day' is another effective way to bring security to the forefront of everyone's mind. Security audits also raise awareness. Consider implementing office space reviews and annual self-assessment surveys.

The key is to make security a part of everyone's day without being obnoxious or repetitive. An awareness programme:

- requires creativity and constant care and attention;

- cannot be conducted in a vacuum;

- must ensure that information security is not seen as something negative but a positive enabler for business.

Finally, management should lead by example: if management believe in information security and they explain their reasoning, it is much easier to bring staff around to the management way of thinking.

6.2.6 Measurement programme

A requirement of ISO/IEC 27001, given in 4.2.2, which falls into the implementation phase, is concerned with measuring the effectiveness of the selected controls or groups of controls. At the implementation stage the company should define how it intends to implement a measurement scheme. It should specify what, when and how measurements are to be taken and used to assess control effectiveness. A starting point can be to identify relevant stakeholders (e.g. customers, senior managers, auditors) and ask them what they care about and how they would judge how well their expectations are met.

Such a scheme should be able to produce comparable and reproducible results. Measuring the effectiveness of controls allows managers and staff to determine how well their controls achieve planned information security objectives. It enables performance levels to be produced which, in turn, helps in assessing how well the company is managing its risks. Like the incident handling process, a measurement scheme is also a valuable management tool. The processes of risk management, incident handling and measurements are three interdependent management tools, which every company would be wise to implement.

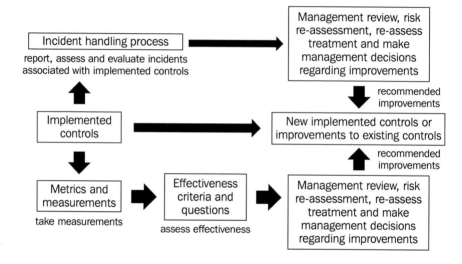

7 Risk Monitoring and Reviews

7.1 Ongoing security risk management

The risk environment of an organization will be in constant change. These changes may affect the organization's risk profile either abruptly or over a period of time. The following are some of the factors that might have an impact on the risks the organization faces:

- new threats and vulnerabilities;

- information security incidents on the increase or decrease;

- new assets have been added to the scope of the ISMS;

- current assets have changed;

- changing business and marketing requirements;

- changes in the workforce;

- restructuring, downsizing, expansion, merging of the business;

- changes to business processes and operations;

- an increase or decrease in the threats and vulnerabilities as a result of the introduction of new technology;

- new legislation, regulations or contractual arrangements;

- an increase in the threats and vulnerabilities as a result of new services deployed;

- changes to outsourcing arrangements that might affect the risk profile.

Each of these factors may have the effect of increasing, or even decreasing, the risks faced by the organization. It is therefore important that the organization regularly monitors and reviews changing circumstances and conditions affecting its business environment, both internal and external changes; such changes may have an impact on its risk and the effectiveness of its current information security management system to cope with any increase in risk.

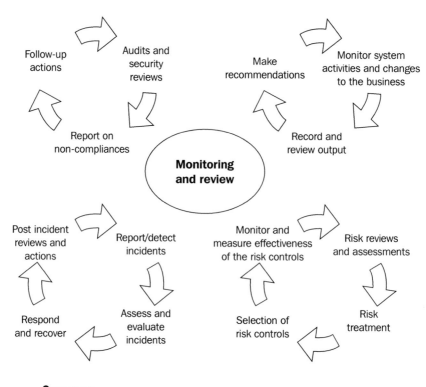

CASE STUDY

An organization decides to outsource the day-to-day management of its business databases to a managed data services company. Its previous information security arrangements will not now cover this revised arrangement; therefore, a reassessment of its risks needs to take place.

For example:

- What is the risk of the outsourcing company being able to protect its customer data?

- What are the risks of the organization being able to access its information across a network connected to the managed data services company?

- What are the service levels provided for such access and availability to its information?

These and many other questions indicate that this management decision to outsource the business databases is very likely to change the risk profile of the organization.

Management of security risk is therefore an ongoing activity that should be assigned to an individual or a team within the organization (ISO/IEC 27001:2005, 5.1). Of course, as part of a contractual arrangement (e.g. with an outsourcing partner) some of the risk may be transferred to the third party to manage; however, the ultimate responsibility for risk management as a whole will still remain in-house.

For a small organization, responsibility may be given to a single individual, as part of a job portfolio. In a larger organization it is likely to be a team of people. In every organization, however, a security manager with responsibility for the ISMS should be clearly identified whether working alone or as part of a team. The person or team managing security risk should have the following characteristics:

- systematic and organized in their approach to monitoring known risks and suggesting appropriate action;

- business-focused and aware of the current state of the business and its priorities;

- tenacious and independently minded, but able to see opposing points of view and accommodate them if it is best for the business;

- able to present a case in a convincing manner to management (e.g. especially where it is a case for expenditure to reduce a high risk);

- able to communicate at all levels in the organization; in particular, able to describe information security issues and status in terms (using language) relevant to the business context or job roles that are important to the organization – in other words, address the 'so what?' question that people may have when they are asked to think about, or take action on, information security;

- a good understanding of risk, and security technology and measures.

7.2 Risk reviews and reassessments

7.2.1 General

The results from an original security risk assessment and management review need to be regularly reviewed for change. There are several factors that could change the risks that were originally assessed. Any new business function could mean new or changed information assets, and any changes documented and considered in the risk assessment and management process. Other changes in the risk situation might occur from a review of the organization, business objectives and/or processes, a review of the correctness and effectiveness of the implemented security controls, and external changes (e.g. environmental, social and political). New or changed threats and/or vulnerabilities may also be identified. After these various changes have been taken into account, the risk should be recalculated and necessary changes to the risk treatment decisions and security controls identified and documented. These changes should be agreed with management and implemented. A risk register should be maintained that includes the date of the last assessment, a description of the risk, an estimate of the impact and the likelihood, any mitigating controls, and a statement of action required, with target date and owner. A maintained risk register provides a useful vehicle for communication (see also Chapter 9) that might arise from publicity about security incidents.

7.2.2 Risk management process reporting and review

The purpose of risk management process reporting and review is to:

- provide the organization with some assurance that the risk management process is operating effectively and risks are being managed, thereby increasing confidence in its ability to achieve objectives and inform decision making;

- enable the organization to aggregate the key risks and issues, and to prioritize and address them appropriately.

Individual risk management process level reporting review should cover:

- the status of key risks surfaced through the process, highlighting any:

  - material changes that could modify their likelihood of occurring and/or their impact; and

  - breach of risk appetite (tolerance or limit);

- the status of mitigating actions for key risks, where progress is behind the agreed target or is significantly threatened; and

- any significant emerging risks that should be raised and monitored.

7.2.3 Inputs into the risk re-assessment

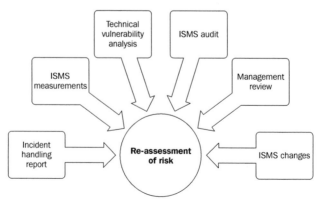

7.2.4 Information security incident management

An information security incident is a very valuable source of information regarding the current level of protection provided by the ISMS. An incident report might indicate, for example:

- new weaknesses in the ISMS not seen, reported or assessed before;

- new threats not experienced before or an increase in the threat level;

- ineffective implementation of a security control or defects in the controls;

- incident impact analysis shows that the potential risk level has increased.

Post-incident analysis should also involve a vulnerability and impact assessment, which can provide important feedback and input to a risk reassessment exercise. Considering the records of incidents over a period of time is also a valuable input into a risk reassessment exercise as it enables an organization to carry out some trend and pattern analysis which may indicate a range of precursors to some future risk problems.

7.2.5 ISMS measurements

One of the key tools available to those responsible for the ISMS is a set of information security metrics and the measurements that have been taken based on these metrics. These are very useful as they can provide an indication of how effective the information security is. These types of metric can be used to set up performance targets to enable organizations to be able to track how well the ISMS is doing with regard to the protection of its assets. The organization can apply metrics and take measurements at different levels:

- management – e.g. decision making, cost–benefit analysis, business impact analysis;

- procedural – e.g. back-ups, information handling, incident handling, access control;

- process – e.g. risk assessment process, audit process, management review process, operational processes;

- technical – e.g. access control system, implementation of network technologies such as firewalls, secure gateways and routers, intrusion detection systems;

- physical – e.g. building, office and room security, equipment.

The following are some example questions related to measurements of the ISMS effectiveness:

1. Is the organization monitoring the ISMS effectiveness in the face of new threats, vulnerabilities, risks and impacts to be taken care of by the ISMS?

2. Is the organization monitoring the ISMS effectiveness in the face of new business requirements (e.g. expansion of its business, using different technologies, embarking on new products, downsizing or upsizing the business or outsourcing part of its business)?

3. Is the organization monitoring the effectiveness of its information security in relation to its business processes?

4. Is the organization monitoring the effectiveness of its staff in how they perform in their job functions and roles in relation to information security? How aware are staff of ISMS policy and how effective is their use of operational procedures?

5. Is the organization monitoring the effectiveness of its incident handling process?

6. How effective is the organization's business continuity plans, disaster recovery process, and its IT readiness capability during a business disruption, disaster or crisis?

Measuring the effectiveness of the ISMS enables the organization to assess and evaluate how good the system of information security controls are at managing the risks it faces. Information security metrics and measurements is a complementary capability alongside risk management that the ISMS team has for ensuring continued protection of the organization's business assets.

7.2.6 Internal and external ISMS audits

Regular internal audits should be scheduled and should be conducted by an independent party (ISO/IEC 27001:2005, 6). The independent party does not need to be from outside the organization. However, audits by an external body are essential for certification under ISO/IEC 27001:2005. Internal auditors should not be under the supervision or control of those responsible for the implementation or daily management of the ISMS. Where internal audits discover a need for action to be taken to adjust the ISMS these should be fully documented, responsibility should be assigned and a target date set. In addition, there may be a need to carry out technical reviews to determine compliance with ISMS policies. Chapter 10 contains further information on audits and reviews of the ISMS.

7.2.7 Business impact analysis (BIA)

The business impact analysis (BIA) is an important aspect of risk review, assessment and reassessment. A BIA should identify impacts resulting from the risks faced by the organization. This may be as a result of the organization's inability to undertake normal business operations caused by, for example, a severe incident event, a disaster, a system failure and so on.

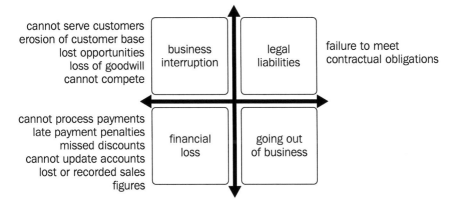

Impacts are measured against particular scenarios – for example, the inability to provide call centre services for a period of time or the loss of network services. The BIA should concentrate on those scenarios where the impact on critical business processes is likely to be greatest. It will include:

- 'hard' impacts – such as financial loss, breach of law, regulations, or standards, failure to achieve agreed service levels, increased costs of working;

- 'soft' impacts – such as political, corporate or personal embarrassment, loss of competitive advantage, loss of image, reputation and business credibility.

It is important to know how the degree of damage or loss is likely to escalate after a service disruption. This will enable the organization to identify the minimum critical requirements for the continued operation of the business, and the timescale within which such requirements should be provided. These requirements include:

- the levels of staffing, skills, facilities and services (including the IT applications and data recovery requirements) necessary to enable critical and essential business processes and operations to continue at a minimum acceptable level;

- the time within which minimum levels of staffing, facilities and services should be recovered;

- the time within which all required business processes, operations and supporting staff, facilities and services should be fully recovered.

The information for a BIA should be collected through interviews or workshops with senior managers of each of the business units. It is important that respondents have a good understanding of their business operations including an appreciation of dependencies on other departments or business units. The BIA enables each business area to understand the point at which the unavailability of its business process or operation would become untenable within the organization: Would the impact take effect immediately, after a day, week, month, or so on? This then allows the most appropriate continuity mechanisms to be determined to meet these business requirements.

The BIA should also consider any implications associated with loss of integrity of information, and for IT systems the impact of the loss of data. With the move to direct data entry and online transaction processing, consideration of how data will be reconciled is an essential part of the recovery process. In most cases, business processes can be re-established without a full complement of staff, systems and other facilities, while still maintaining an acceptable level of service to clients and customers. The business recovery objectives should therefore be stated in terms of:

- the time within which a predefined team of core staff and stated minimum facilities must be recovered (RTO);

- the timetable for recovery of remaining staff and facilities;

- the point to which data must be recovered (RPO).

Effect rating

Value	Rating	Definition
0.0	None	No effect on the business
0.1	Minimal	Negligible effect on the business
0.25	Low	Moderate effect
0.5	Medium	Severe effect on part of the business and moderate effect on the business overall
0.75	High	Severe effect on multiple parts of the business
1.0	Critical	Severe effect on the whole business leading to a major crisis or emergency

Criticality rating

Value	Rating	Definition
0.1	Minimal	Non-critical systems
0.25	Low	System or systems that support a part of the business but not mission critical
0.5	Medium	System or systems that support a part of the business that is mission critical
0.75	High	System or systems that support multiple parts of the business that are mission critical
1.0	Critical	System or systems that are mission critical and support the whole business

Incident impact rating

Score	Rating
0.00–0.99	None
1.00–2.49	Minimal
2.50–3.74	Low
3.75–4.99	Medium
5.00–7.49	High
7.50–10.00	Critical

Using the rating and the criticality tables an organization can determine the overall severity rating for an incident; organizations should use the following formula:

Overall severity/Effect score =

Round ((Current effect rating * 2.5) + (Projected effect rating *2.5) + (System criticality rating * 5))

7.2.8 Management reviews

Management need to review the ISMS to ensure its continuing suitability, adequacy and effectiveness. In order to ensure the adequacy of the ISMS, management need to consider the changing risk situation and the ability of the ISMS to deal with these changed risks. The scope of the ISMS might require redefinition as a result of changed business objectives or other important modifications. Regular management reviews should take place. Organizations should tune the ISMS by reviewing appropriate targets and metrics. Either qualitative or quantitative targets could be appropriate, depending on the nature of the ISMS.

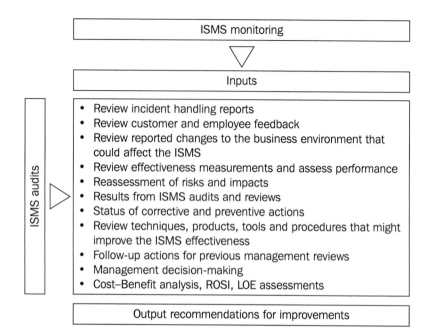

Reviews should be based on information from users of the ISMS, results from previous reviews, audit reports, records of procedures, and internal and external benchmarking. The output of the review should be specific about changes to the ISMS – for example, by identifying modifications to procedures that affect information security, and to ensure adequacy of coverage. The output should also show where efficiency improvements can be made. The review should be clear about required resources, both to implement the improvements and to maintain them.

7.2.9 Feedback and involvement

Feedback is an essential ingredient in making an ISMS more effective. The aim is to ensure that the ISMS becomes part of the organizational culture. The identification and reporting of problems, increased risks and security incidents should be encouraged. Effective suggestions for remediation strategies should be rewarded. These should be collected and evaluated systematically (for example, an employee suggestion form could be used). The following suggests how a feedback and involvement process should be conducted.

1. Use a suggestion form or scorecard that is simple and easy to complete.

2. Define a clear scope for suggestions focusing on the ISMS and related business activities.

3. Identify contacts for suggestions, questions and queries.

4. Acknowledge all input.

5. Keep an open mind and be flexible about suggestions.

6. Involve the person who made the suggestion in the problem solving process, where possible.

7. Provide a reward system for useful input.

8. Implement suggested improvements quickly and effectively.

9. Publicize successful improvements.

10. Issue periodic reminders about the improvement process.

An effective ISMS needs to draw information from all possible sources, including management and all employees and contractors, irrespective of their function, as well as people from outside such as outsourcers, suppliers and customers, where relevant. Participating in the ISMS improvement process should be part of every employee's job description.

7.2.10 ISMS changes

There may be organizational changes that change the scope of the ISMS. For example, an organization may merge its business operations with another organization, or it may outsource some of its operations. It might restructure, downsize or expand its operations, its areas of business and its workforce. The ISMS may grow to cover more than one part of the business. All of these scenarios have the effect of changing the assets included in the scope. The following examples illustrate some of these scenarios.

Assets

There are various types of change that might have a risk impact on the business assets the organization has, for example:

- broader ISMS scope;
- more staff;
- more locations and sites;
- more information systems;
- acquisition of new information;
- information becomes more or less sensitive and/or more or less critical;
- information needs to be more available;
- a legacy system or process becomes less important as a result of the introduction of new technology;

- introduction of new technology, services or processes;
- greater market share;
- change in the market or share value of the business;
- business mergers
- depreciation in equipment values.

Company mergers

A new company is formed by the merger of two existing companies.

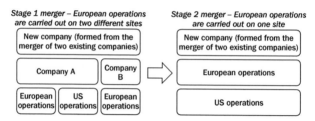

Prior to the merger the only implemented ISMS was the European operations of Company A. Post-merger it is decided by management to expand the scope of the ISMS to cover the European operations of both Company A and Company B. In Stage 1 of the merger the ISMS will cover two different sites, but in Stage 2 of the merger all European operations will be carried out on one site.

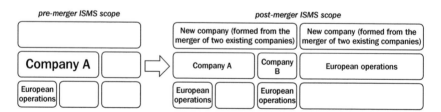

A checklist of risk assessment activities to be done would include:

1. Update asset inventory for the new ISMS.

2. Review the policies, procedures and existing controls for Company B.

3. Review the risk assessments from Company B and any other risk-related documents, processes or activities.

4. Carry out a risk assessment for the Stage 1 merger.

5. Implement the necessary controls for the two sites – monitoring and review their effectiveness;

6. Prior to the Stage 2 merger carry out a further risk assessment and then implement any necessary additional controls for the new combined operations.

Internal expansion of scope

This is an example of a company that designs and develops a range of software for different industries in the safety sector. The current ISMS scope covers the software testing and evaluation project group.

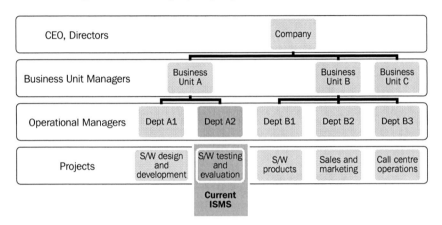

Senior management decides to expand the scope of the ISMS to include the software design and development project group after an increase in the number of regulatory controls, applicable to the safety industry, with which they now need to comply and which included requirements for information security. This entails a reassessment of the risks to take account of the increase in the number of assets as well as a whole range of new threats and vulnerabilities not previously considered in the original scope.

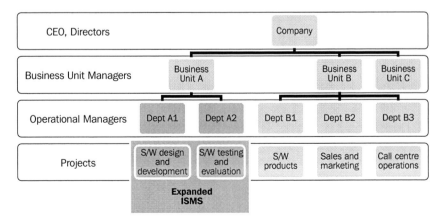

Threat and vulnerability changes

The organization might have changes to its threat profile as a result of:

- greater connectivity;

- greater use of mobile and wireless networking;

- greater online business being deployed;

- more remote working arrangements;

- information needs to be more available;

- introduction of new technology;

- more outsourcing arrangements introduced;

- greater number of untrained workforce.

These changes to the organization may introduce a greater number of vulnerabilities and hence increase the potential number of risks it faces.

7.3 Monitoring system and resource usage

Procedures for monitoring the use of information processing facilities should be established and the results of the monitoring activities reviewed regularly. How often these results are reviewed should depend on the risks involved. Risk factors that should be considered include the:

- criticality of the application processes and services;

- value, sensitivity, and criticality of the information involved;

- past experience of system infiltration and misuse, and the frequency of vulnerabilities being exploited;

- past experience of system bugs, performance problems, failures and errors, and the frequency of vulnerabilities being exploited;

- extent of system networking and interconnections (particularly public networks);

- logging facility being de-activated.

Monitoring and reviewing the acceptable use of organizational resources, given the high level of incidents that are caused by the insider threat, whether intentional or accidental, should take place in any circumstances as this is essential in any effective ISMS implementation (see ISO/IEC 27001).

Monitoring and review measures should be in place at different levels within the organization:

- human resources level – e.g. awareness and training, day-to-day working practices, records of user errors, incident handling reports indicating human resources security problems;

- Process, policy and procedural level;

- Technical level – e.g. through the use of system logs, audit trails, monitoring software.

CASE STUDY

A European publishing company decides to deploy an *acceptable use policy* (AUP) throughout its business. The purpose and objective of this policy is to prevent damaging the image of the company through the use of its email system. This policy covers appropriate use of any email sent from the company's email system and applies to all employees, service providers and agents operating on behalf of the company. Requiring each employee to sign a copy of the policy enables the company, in accordance with certain legal conventions, to monitor their use of the company's email system, using current available technology. The following are some of the clauses that such an AUP might contain:

Policy Prohibited Use: The company email system shall not to be used for the creation or distribution of any disruptive or offensive messages, including offensive comments about a person's race, gender, religion, disabilities or age. Also prohibited is the use of emails of a sexual and pornographic nature, or which contain religious and/or political beliefs. Staff who receive any emails of this type, from any other member of staff or from outside sources, should report the matter to their manager immediately.

Personal Use: The company allows a reasonable amount of its email resources to be used for personal use as long as such use does not interfere with the user's normal work tasks and the company's day-to-day operations and customer services. Any non-work related emails and attachments shall be saved in a separate folder from work-related email. However, the sending of chain letters or joke emails from the company email account is prohibited. Before sending mailings via a distribution list from the company, such mailings shall be approved by the head of the company operations. These restrictions also apply to the forwarding of mail received by a company member of staff.

> **Monitoring Email Usage:** The company reserves the right to monitor email system usage and to check anything that is stored, sent or received via the email system without prior notice. Therefore members of staff should not expect any privacy protection from the company's email system.
>
> **Disciplinary Action:** Any member of staff who violates this policy may be subject to disciplinary action. Depending on the severity of the resulting security policy violation the action may include termination of employment.

7.4 Monitoring and review of external services

External services deployed by an organization are subject to change. With outsourcing, for example, the following might become areas of change:

- Contracts and SLAs may need to be amended as a result of changes by either party in the outsourcing arrangement.

- The quality and levels of service may increase or decrease.

- The levels of risk associated with the outsourcing arrangement might increase or decrease.

- The service provider may experience various changes (e.g. organizational changes, changes to location, resourcing problems, subcontracts).

The organization may deploy a wide range of external services all of which need to be part of the ongoing management activity of monitoring and review of changes that might affect the risk profile of the organization. Some of the external services an organization might deploy are:

- service providers, such as ISPs, network providers, telephone services, maintenance and support services;

- managed security services;

- outsourcing of facilities and/or operations, e.g. IT systems, data collection services, call centre operations;

- management and business consultants, and auditors;

- developers and suppliers, e.g. of software products and IT systems;

- cleaning, catering, and other outsourced support services;

- temporary personnel, student placement, and other casual short-term appointments.

7.5 Monitoring system of controls

Implemented security controls should be regularly monitored and reviewed to ensure that they function correctly and effectively and that changes in the environment have not rendered them ineffective (see also ISO/IEC 27001:2005, 4.2.3). Over time there is a tendency for the performance of any service or mechanism to deteriorate. Monitoring is intended to detect this deterioration and initiate corrective action.

The majority of security controls will require maintenance and administrative support to ensure their correct and appropriate functioning during their life. These activities should be planned and performed on a regular, scheduled basis. In this manner their overheads can be minimized, and the relevance of the security controls preserved.

Maintenance activities include:

* checking that controls are implemented and configured as specified (i.e. that things are as they are thought to be);

* checking log files;

* modifying parameters to reflect changes and additions;

* reviewing controls and compliance with them;

* updating controls, policies and procedures with new versions.

Many controls produce an output that should be checked for security significant events; these include logs, alarm reports, incident management reports, vulnerability management processes, and application reviews.

General system audit functions can provide useful information, which can be used in this regard. Automated review and analysis of system logs, or a secondary human review, is an effective tool for helping to ensure the intended performance.

8 Risk Control Improvements

8.1 Non-conformities

A management system non-conformity is a failure to conform to the requirements of a management system standard – for example, any of the 'shall' requirements of ISO/IEC 27001. The degree of non-conformity indicates the severity of the potential risk the organization faces by not complying with the requirements of ISO/IEC 27001.

Major non-conformities
Those that could cause a major risk and impact to the company, which need to be dealt with immediately.

Minor non-conformities
Those that could cause a minor risk and impact to the company; which do not need immediate attention but will be considered in the future.

8.2 Corrective and preventive actions

8.2.1 Objectives

Correction: action to eliminate a detected non-conformity

Corrective action: action to eliminate the cause of a detected non-conformity or other undesirable situation

Both correction and corrective action should be expected when there is a non-conformity is detected. *Correction* is action to eliminate a detected non-conformity. Correction may involve, for example, replacing non-conforming product with conforming product or replacing an obsolete procedure with the current issue, etc.

The definition of *corrective action* is 'action to eliminate the cause of a detected non-conformity'. Corrective action cannot be taken without first making a determination of the cause of non-conformity.

Effective corrective action should prevent the recurrence of the non-conformity by eliminating the cause. However, corrective action should not be confused with preventive action. The definition for preventive action is as follows:

Preventive action: action to eliminate the cause of a potential non-conformity or other undesirable situation

It should be noted that preventive action, by the nature of its definition, is not applicable to non-conformities that have already been detected. However, an analysis of the causes of detected non-conformities may identify potential non-conformities on a wider scale in other areas of the organization and provide input for preventive action.

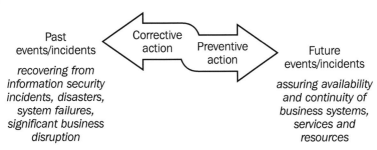

8.2.2 Implementation guidance

Action should be taken as a result of monitoring, reviews and audits (ISO/IEC 27001:2005, 8.2, 8.3). These actions need to be verified independently to ensure that they:

- relate to the identified root cause and appropriately address the problem;

- have actually been implemented;

- are effective in preventing a recurrence of the problem.

The verification evidence needed might require a repetition of the 'Plan-Do-Check-Act' cycle. Thus an accurate picture of the efficacy of corrective and preventative action will be built over time.

8.3 Implement the identified improvements in the ISMS

8.3.1 Objective

Any improvements identified during the 'Check phase' of the risk management process (see Chapter 7 above) will need to be implemented and deployed during the 'Act phase' of the risk management process. This is a time when corrective and preventive actions (8.2) need to be carried out. These actions will have been driven by a risk review and reassessment during the 'Check phase'. The risk review might have been triggered by an incident, system failure or disaster that may have happened as a result of a set of measurements that were taken to check the effectiveness of the information security, or as a result of changes to the business and how it operates. These corrective and preventive actions may result in the organization being required to implement new controls or improve existing controls, or a combination of these two options.

8.3.2 Case studies

The following are some case study examples of making improvements.

8.3.2.1 Policies and procedures

Updating and revising existing policies and procedures is one area of improvement that can be undertaken:

CASE STUDY

Backup procedures and processes are found to be ineffective to deal with system recovery and cleanups following a major DoS (denial of service) incident. What improvements could be made? Examples:

- more specific information and clearer instructions on how to deal with crisis and emergency situations;

- the approach and process of taking backups, recovery of backups, use in system close down and start-up needs to be improved and tested;

- better training in using backup procedures and the process.

CASE STUDY

Information handling procedures are found to be inadequate and not sufficiently effective to deal with access by third parties with outsourcing arrangements. What improvements could be made? Examples:

- a review of the risks involved and translation of this knowledge into improvements in procedures to be applied to information that is outsourced or accessible by third parties;

- review and improve the access control and acceptable use policy;

- revise the information classification scheme.

CASE STUDY

The policy on the use of mobile technology and remote access for staff is inadequate following several misuses of privileges as indicated by customer complaints concerning staff working on customers' sites. What improvements could be made? Examples:

- greater restrictions on the use of such technology and remote access;

- more effective controls for remote working;

- better training on the use of policies and procedures regarding the use of such technology;

- appropriate disciplinary action to be taken against staff who are found to be misusing rights, privileges and company resources.

8.3.2.2 Technical controls

Revisiting and updating existing technical controls is one area of improvement that can be undertaken:

CASE STUDY

The current set of access methods for network services needs to be improved following a number of successful attempts by staff to gain access to sites they are not supposed to access. Information about this situation was obtained while handling two recent incidents and this information was corroborated with measurements taken. What improvements could be made? Examples:

- more effective network monitoring and control of access;

- stronger deterrents and methods of denying access;

- consideration of different access technology;

- improve the disciplinary process and create greater awareness of this process.

8.3.2.3 Management and planning

Management and planning controls is one area of improvement that can be undertaken:

CASE STUDY

The capacity of system resources is found to be inadequate and ineffective to deal with the varying business demands and changes including outsourcing arrangements. This has recently resulted in several system crashes and system downtimes causing a loss of availability. What improvements could be made? Examples:

- improve understanding of the business requirements and demands on system resources by more regular reviews;

- improve the capacity of system resources;

- increase the frequency of capacity planning exercises.

8.4 Ensure that the improvements achieve their intended objectives

8.4.1 Objective

Once improvements to the information security controls have been made, the next task is to make sure the improvements do what they are expected to do and check that the improvement objectives have been met. If a procedure was revised to improve its user-friendliness and applicability, the organization needs to check that these objectives have been met.

8.4.2 Implementation guidance

Part of the task in checking that the improvements do what they are expected to do is through awareness and training exercises, as well as looking at how staff deal with the controls in their day-to-day work routines: Are they applying the new controls correctly? Are the staff having difficulty using the new controls? Are the staff finding any problems or weaknesses with the controls?

Another aspect of checking that the improvements do what they are expected to do is through testing that the technical controls work correctly: Does the new password regime work or can it be compromised? Do the new physical controls work as they should do? Are the access control methods robust enough to withstand attack?

A further aspect of verification is to check that the new or revised processes do what they are expected to do: Do improvements to the incident handling process meet expectations? Is the new backup process proving to work as expected? Is the disaster recovery process meeting expectations?

Ideally controls should not be deployed in an operational environment until they have undergone some form of testing and verification to check that they are ready to be operationally deployed. Of course, this may not be the case with all controls.

It is not out of the question to engage the information security measurement process in the verification exercises.

8.5 Communicate the actions and improvements

8.5.1 Objective

Like many other aspects of good management practice, communication is as essential during the improvement process as it is during all the other information security processes. Lack of communication is a risk in itself. Communication covers a variety of aspects including:

- informing staff that new or revised policies and procedures are now to be used and where they can obtain access to these new or revised versions;

- staff awareness of new or revised working methods and practices, and the provisioning of appropriate training where necessary and appropriate;

- informing staff of new or revised reporting practices and channels regarding information security incidents, weaknesses and other information security-related events.

Regularly reporting and reviewing key risks identified through each application of the risk management process is fundamental to the organization's ability to:

- actively manage risk;

- aggregate and profile its risk status; and

- monitor and respond to changes in risk profile at all levels and across the organization.

8.5.2 Communication plan

An ISMS requires co-operation with, and input by, all levels and functions of the organization (ISO/IEC 27001:2005, 7.2). Effective risk reporting and communication are therefore essential.

A communication plan should be established, which identifies key players and decision-makers as well as mechanisms for disseminating decisions and for collecting feedback (see 7.2.8 to 7.2.9). The plan should include mechanisms for regular updating of risk information as part of the ongoing security awareness programme. It should also include procedures for dealing with public relations issues.

9 Documentation System

9.1 General

Complete, accessible and correct documentation and a controlled process to manage documents are necessary to support the ISMS, although the scope and detail will vary between organizations. Responsibility for overseeing the process of managing documentation needs to be clearly assigned and agreed.

Documentation includes policies, standards, guidelines, procedures, checklists, the risk register and other guidance in support of the ISMS. A list of required documentation can be found in ISO/IEC 27001:2005, 4.3.1. These documents, and any other documentation and records that are necessary to operate the ISMS and to provide evidence that the ISMS is operating correctly and efficiently, should be maintained, and should be current and relevant. Some documentation, which is relevant to enforcing the ISMS controls, will be more generally applicable to all employees and their job functions other as opposed to those documents that are applicable to those specifically responsible for information security. Documentation controls which apply to the ISMS should also apply equally to security documentation which is embedded somewhere outside the ISMS.

The requirements for documentation and record control are contained in ISO/IEC 27001:2005, 4.3.2 and 4.3.3. These requirements are directly aligned with the documentation requirements of other management systems, such as ISO 9001:2000. These aligned requirements help to combine different management systems and to consistently apply necessary documentation control. Effective document control also supports consistent dissemination of information, while removing the potential for confusion over the state of the ISMS at any point.

9.2 Risk report

As the name suggests, the risk report should document all the necessary information regarding risk assessment that has been carried out. There are no specific ISO/IEC guidelines setting out what such a report should look like or what it should contain. What is suggested here is one or several ways in which to view a risk report. It is suggested here that the report may contain the following:

- an outline of the risk approach taken;

- the criteria used for levels of risk acceptance and risk residuals;

- the evaluation scales used for the assets, threats, vulnerabilities and impacts;

- the scope of the assessment;

- how the assessment was conducted and who was involved;

- a risk register;

- a risk treatment plan;

- statement of applicability;

- summary and conclusions.

9.2.1 Risk register

It is important to have a risk register as a record of the results of the risk assessment. The risks listed on this register should be in priority order with the highest risks grouped at the top of the register and the low risks grouped together at the bottom. This register is a 'living document' in the sense that it will need to be reviewed and updated on a regular basis. This register should also be linked to the risk treatment plan, which again is a 'living document'.

CASE STUDY

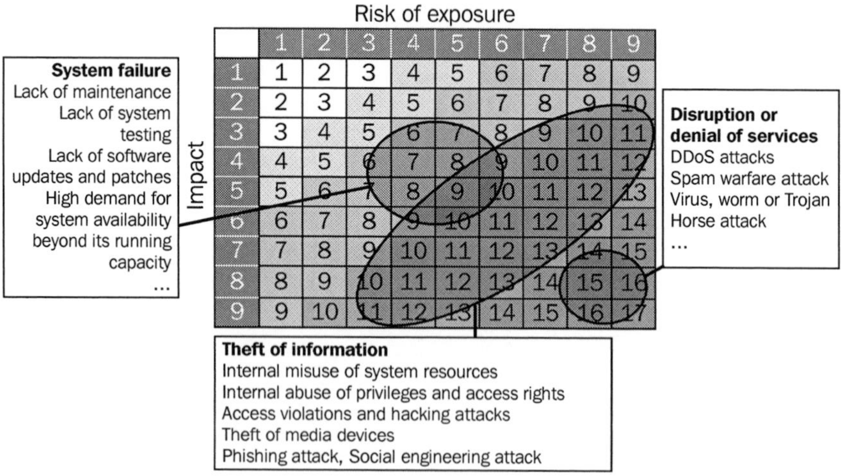

Risk of exposure

		1	2	3	4	5	6	7	8	9	
System failure	1	1	2	3	4	5	6	7	8	9	
Lack of maintenance Lack of system testing	2	2	3	4	5	6	7	8	9	10	**Disruption or denial of services**
Lack of software updates and patches	3	3	4	5	6	7	8	9	10	11	DDoS attacks
	4	4	5	6	7	8	9	10	11	12	Spam warfare attack
High demand for system availability beyond its running capacity	5	5	6	7	8	9	10	11	12	13	Virus, worm or Trojan Horse attack
	6	6	7	8	9	10	11	12	13	14	...
	7	7	8	9	10	11	12	13	14	15	
	8	8	9	10	11	12	13	14	15	16	
	9	9	10	11	12	13	14	15	16	17	

(Impact is the vertical axis label on the left.)

Theft of information
Internal misuse of system resources
Internal abuse of privileges and access rights
Access violations and hacking attacks
Theft of media devices
Phishing attack, Social engineering attack

Risk name/type	Level of risk	Details of the cause of the risk
Denial of service	very high (14–17)	No protection in place against spam and DDoS/Botnet attacks, no business continuity in place, out of date protection against malicious code
Theft of information	high (10–13)	Internal misuse of IT resources, abuse of access rights and privileges, access violations, theft of media
System failure	medium (6–9)	Lack of system maintenance, lack of system testing, out of date patches and software upgrades, operational demands beyond system capacity

9.2.2 Statement of Applicability

The Statement of Applicability (SoA) provides a summary of decisions concerning risk treatment and the control objectives and controls that have been selected for implementation. The SoA should justify any excluded controls thus providing a cross-check that no controls have been inadvertently omitted. As a mandatory requirement of ISO/IEC 27001:2005, a SoA must be prepared that includes the following:

- the control objectives and controls selected and the reasons for their selection;

- the control objectives and controls currently implemented; and

- the exclusion of any control objectives and controls and the justification for their exclusion.

The SoA is a very important document for those organizations that have their ISMS certified.

Annex A Control Objective	Annex A Control	Selected/ currently implemented	Reason for selection/justification for exclusion
A.5.1 Information security policy	A.5.1.1 Information security policy document		
	A.5.1.2 Review of the information security policy		
A.6.1 Internal organization	A.6.1.1 Management commitment to information security		
	A.6.1.2 Information security co-ordination		
	A.6.1.3 Allocation of information security responsibilities		
A.6.2 External parties			
A.15.3 Information systems audit considerations			

9.2.3 Case study

The following table illustrates an example of how one company presented the results of its risk assessment and the selection of controls process.

Risk	Threat/vulnerability source	Existing controls	Likelihood	Impact level	Risk rating/level	Recommended controls
User system passwords can be guessed or cracked	Hackers/password effectiveness	Passwords must be alphanumeric and at least 8 characters in length	medium	medium	medium	Require use of special characters
Web server and application server running unnecessary services	All/unnecessary services	None	medium	medium	medium	Reconfigure systems to remove unnecessary services
DDoS attack	Network access to untrusted sites, volume of spam traffic, and so on	None	medium	high	high	

9.2.4 Risk treatment plan

Once the risk treatment decisions have been taken, the activities to implement these decisions need to be identified and planned. Each implementation activity should be clearly identified and broken into as many sub-activities as are needed to be able to allocate clear responsibilities to individuals, estimate resource requirements, set milestones and deadlines, identify deliverables and monitor progress.

The planning process needs to include the identification of key stakeholders, such as resource owners, and a consultation process to ensure that resource requirements are properly estimated and can be made available, and that the relevant levels of management approval to spend the resources have been obtained. The time when each activity can be undertaken depends on the overall priority in relation to the other activities in the programme, the resource availability (including consideration of funding and availability of people) and whether it is dependent on any other activity to be completed before the process can be started. Other business and IT change programmes of work will usually have to be carefully co-ordinated with the risk treatment plan to ensure that any dependencies are identified and taken into account.

Prioritizing activities is a management function and is usually closely aligned with the risk assessment activity discussed in Chapter 5. Priorities for action are usually set to ensure that activity is focused on the largest risks, though other political processes might also influence these priorities, such as the need to demonstrate quick wins to senior management.

In summary, the following activities need to be undertaken when formulating a risk treatment plan:

- limiting factors and dependencies should be identified;
- priorities should be established;
- deadlines should be identified and milestones should be agreed;
- resource requirements should be estimated and resources identified;
- approvals to spend or allocate resources should be obtained;
- the critical path should be identified.

Once the risk treatment plan has been formulated, resources can be allocated and activity to implement the risk management decisions can be started. It is necessary at this stage to ensure that there is a clear review process in place to ensure that activity is undertaken as planned, that deliverables are of the desired quality, that milestones are met and that resource estimates are not exceeded (see also 7.3). The risk treatment plan, as mentioned earlier, is a 'living document'. It should enable those responsible for managing the implementation to keep track of the status of implementation and the effect that the risk controls are having on managing the risks. Again, it is useful to link this with the risk register, which as a 'living document' provides a profile for the company of its current risk position.

9.3 Electronic documentation system

There are various benefits from having all the ISMS-related documents – such as policies and procedures, guidance and handbooks, training and awareness material, forms for reporting incidents and so on – available in electronic form in a central server on the company's internal network. Benefits include:

- improved accessibility and faster retrieval time – obtaining paper from storage or an archive is typically slower than electronic access and retrieval of documentation;

- along with the improved retrieval time comes the ability to perform searches for similar information, which is especially useful when trying to perform major changes or perhaps searching for information subject to litigation;

- reduced need to print paper documents as electronic versions are available for use or reuse – this saves paper, printer and toner costs;

- improved staff productivity since employees spend less time searching for documents or trying to find the current version;

- faster distribution of documents – new, revisions and updates;

- faster document review and approval cycles, particularly where multiple reviews and approvals are involved in the business process.

The commonly expressed adage 'lose your records and you lose your business' illustrates the need to have a secure documentation system. Some of the information security benefits of having an electronic documentation system include:

- improved security through a single secure location for documents and ensuring that the right people are able to access the right documents;

- improved compliance with regulation or legislation;

- central control and management of documentation;

- improvements in data backup and recovery;

- greatly assists in any disaster recovery, incident handling or business continuity event;

- reduced chance of 'losing' documents;

- improvements in internal document processes;

- improved customer service through faster access to and retrieval of important customer information.

10 Audits and Reviews

10.1 Internal ISMS audits

An internal ISMS audit is a mandatory requirement of ISO/IEC 27001:2005 (4.2.3 e) and is part of the monitoring and review (Check phase) process that was covered in Chapter 7 and Chapter 8 of this book.

The purpose of conducting an internal ISMS audit is to determine whether the control objectives, controls, processes and procedures of the ISMS:

- conform to the requirements of ISO/IEC 27001:2005 and relevant legislation or regulations;

- conform to the identified information security requirements of the company;

- are effectively implemented and maintained and perform as expected.

Internal ISMS audits should be carried out on a regular basis – perhaps every six, nine or twelve months.

Internal ISMS auditors cannot audit their own work; so, for example, those in charge of the design, implementation and maintenance of the ISMS are not permitted to carry out such an audit. The internal ISMS auditors are required to carry out the audit process in the same way in which other management system audits are carried out. An audit programme is to be planned, taking into consideration the status and importance of the processes and areas to be audited as well as the results of previous audits; the audit criteria, scope, frequency and methods are to be defined and the selection of auditors and conduct of audits must ensure objectivity and impartiality of the audit process (see ISO 19011 for more details of the general process). ISO/IEC 27007 provides the relevant auditor guidance in respect of the information security specifics of internal ISMS audits.

As regards the results of the internal ISMS audit, the management in the part of the organization who are responsible for the area being audited are required to ensure that actions are taken without undue delay to eliminate detected non-conformities and their causes. Follow-up activities are to include verification of the actions taken and reporting of the verification results.

10.2 External ISMS audits

10.2.1 General

An external ISMS audit is not a mandatory requirement of ISO/IEC 27001:2005 and it is for each individual organization to decide whether or not it has such an audit. These audits are carried out by third party auditing companies, commonly referred to as certification bodies. Not all auditing companies are certification bodies in the sense that they have undergone a formal accreditation process carried out by a national accreditation body (see 10.2.2). As with internal ISMS audits, general guidance for auditors is provided by ISO 19011 and more specific guidance is provided by ISO/IEC 27007.

Third party certification ISMS audits provide an organization and its customers with an assurance that its information security management system met the requirements of ISO/IEC 27001:2005 at the time of certification and that its system is being systematically reviewed. The value of ISMS certification is the degree of public confidence and trust that is established by an impartial and competent audit by the certification body. There are various reasons why an organization will choose certification, for example:

- it provides assurance to its customers, business partners and shareholders that it is 'fit for purpose' to operate its business securely, e.g. in providing outsourcing services;

- its customers require it to be compliant;

- to comply with legislation, e.g. demonstrating that the organization complies with data protection/privacy legislation;

- to demonstrate that it is managing its risks and it has appropriate governance controls in place;

- as a market differentiator in comparison with its competitors.

10.2.2 Players

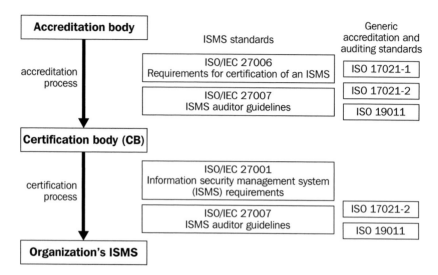

The following figure shows the roles of the accreditation body assessor teams and the certification body audit teams.

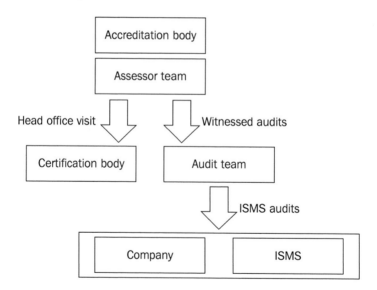

10.3 Audit process

10.3.1 Scope of audit

An organization should define the scope of its ISMS. The role of the certification body (CB) is to confirm that the ISMS scope is well defined, clear, complete and consistent, and to check that nothing is excluded from the scope of the ISMS elements of the organization's operation which should properly be included within it.

The CB should therefore ensure that the organization's information security risk assessment properly reflects its activities and extends to the boundaries of its activities as defined in the ISMS standard or normative document. The CB should confirm that this is reflected in the organization's information Statement of Applicability (SoA).

The SoA will be a documented statement describing the control objectives and controls that are relevant and applicable to the organization's ISMS. Control objectives and controls are based on the results and conclusions of the risk assessment and risk treatment processes, legal or regulatory requirements, contractual obligations and the organization's business requirements for information security.

NOTE: Any exclusion of controls found to be necessary to satisfy the risk acceptance criteria must be justified and evidence must be provided that the associated risks have been accepted by accountable persons. Where any controls are excluded, claims of conformity to ISO/IEC 27001:2005 are not acceptable unless such exclusions do not affect the organization's ability, and/or responsibility, to provide information security that meets the security requirements determined by risk assessment and applicable legal or regulatory requirements.

Interfaces with services or activities that are not completely within the scope of the ISMS should be addressed within the ISMS subject to certification and should be included in the organization's information security risk assessment. An example of such a situation is the sharing of facilities (e.g. computers, telecommunication systems, and so on) with others.

10.3.2 Audit stages

The following is a description of the ISO/IEC 27001:2005 general two-stage process:

Stage 1 audit

At this stage of the audit, the certification body (CB) should obtain documentation relating to the design of the ISMS covering at least the company's analysis of information security-related risks, the Statement of Applicability, and the core elements of the ISMS.

The objectives of the Stage 1 audit are to provide a focus for planning the Stage 2 audit by gaining an understanding of the ISMS in the context of the organization's security policy and objectives and, in particular, of the organization's state of preparedness for the audit.

The Stage 1 audit includes, but should not be restricted to, the document review. The CB and the company are to agree when and where the document review is conducted. In every case, the document review should be completed prior to the start of the Stage 2 audit. The results of the Stage 1 audit should be documented in a written report. The CB should review the Stage 1 audit report to decide whether to proceed with the Stage 2 audit and for selecting the Stage 2 audit team members with the necessary competence. The CB should make the company aware of the further types of information and records that may be required for detailed inspection during the Stage 2 audit. When the Stage 1 audit, including the document review, is not conducted by a single person the CB should be able to demonstrate how the activities of the various team members are co-ordinated.

Stage 2 audit

The Stage 2 audit always takes place at the site(s) of the organization. On the basis of findings documented in the Stage 1 audit report, the audit team drafts an audit plan for the conduct of the Stage 2 audit. The objectives of this audit are:

- to confirm that the organization adheres to its own policies, objectives and procedures;

- to confirm that the ISMS conforms with all the requirements of the ISMS standard or normative document and is achieving the organization's policy objectives.

In order to do this, the certification body's audit team will focus on the organization's:

- assessment of information security-related risks and the resulting design and development of the ISMS;

- Statement of Applicability;

- objectives and targets derived from this ISMS risk and design process;

- performance monitoring, measuring, reporting and reviewing against the objectives and targets;

- security and management reviews;

- management responsibility for the information security policy;

- links between the ISMS policy, the results of information security risk assessments, objectives and targets, responsibilities, programmes, procedures, performance data, and security reviews.

Specific elements of the ISMS audit

The role of the certification body is to check how the company has evaluated the information security-related threats to assets, vulnerabilities, risks and impacts on the company and how it has implemented controls to manage those risks that are deemed to be significant. In order to provide confidence that the organization is consistent in establishing and maintaining procedures for the identification, examination and evaluation of information security-related threats to assets, vulnerabilities and impacts on the organization, certification bodies should consider the following factors:

- It is for the company to define the criteria by which information security-related threats to assets, vulnerabilities and impacts on the company are identified as being significant, and to develop procedure(s) for doing this.

- The certification body should require the company to demonstrate that the analysis of security-related threats is relevant and adequate for the operation of the company.

- Is there any inconsistency between the organization's policy, objectives and targets and its procedure(s) or the results of its application?

The certification body should establish whether the procedures employed in analysis of significance are sound and properly implemented. If an information security-related threat to the assets and/or an impact on the company is identified as being significant, it should be managed within the ISMS.

Surveillance audits

The ISMS certificate awarded to the company lasts for three years after which the certificate can be renewed based on a successful reassessment of its ISMS. As a minimum, surveillance by the certification body of the organization's ISMS will take place on an annual basis. Sometimes certification bodies might carry out two surveillance audits a year.

The purpose of these surveillance audits is to check that:

- the effectiveness of the ISMS with regard to achieving the objectives of the organization's information security policy is being maintained;

- the functioning of procedures for the periodic evaluation and review of compliance with relevant information security legislation and regulations are working;

- action taken on non-conformities identified during the last audit have been dealt with.

The certification body should be able to adapt its surveillance programme to the information security-related threats to assets, vulnerabilities, risks and impacts that the organization has had to deal with between successive audits. The surveillance audit programme will be determined by the certification body who will agree the specific dates for visits with the organization beforehand. The audit methodology for reassessments should be the same as for the initial audit.

10.3.3 Documents

The ISMS documentation required for a certification audit shall include:

• documented statements of the ISMS policy and objectives;

• the scope of the ISMS;

• procedures and controls in support of the ISMS;

• a description of the risk assessment methodology;

• the risk assessment report (see 9.2);

• the risk treatment plan (see 9.2.4);

• documented procedures required by the organization to ensure the effective planning, operation and control of its information security processes and describe how to measure the effectiveness of controls;

• records required by ISO/IEC 27001:2005; and

• the Statement of Applicability (see 9.2.2).

10.3.4 Audit report and award of certificate

Reporting by audit teams to the certification body

In order to provide a basis for the certification decision, the certification body will require clear audits reports from its audit team, which provide sufficient information to arrive at the decision.

Reports from the audit team to the certification body are required at various stages in the assessment process. These reports will contain at least:

• an account of the audit including a summary of the document review;

• an account of the assessment of the organization's information security risk assessment;

• the total audit time used and a detailed specification of the time spent on document review, assessment of risk analysis, implementation audit, and audit reporting;

• clarification of non-conformities;

- audit enquiries which have been followed, rationale for their selection, and the methodology employed;

- recommendation on certification by the audit team to the certification body.

Decision making

The person(s) in the certification body entity who takes the decision on granting or withdrawing a certification will have a level of knowledge and experience in all areas which is sufficient to evaluate the audit processes, the report and associated recommendations made by the audit team. The person(s) making the decision will not have been part of the audit team.

11 Standards

11.1 General

The following is a brief taxonomy of ISO/IEC 27001:2005 relevant standards and guidelines. It includes international standards published by ISO/IEC as well as regional standards and guidelines provided by industry groups and associations.

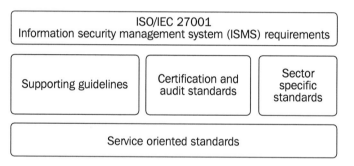

The standards and guidelines listed below all support the implementation of ISO/IEC 27001:2005. Some of the ISO standards listed have been published; others are in the process of being developed.

11.2 Security controls

Published

- ISO/IEC 27001:2005 Information technology – Security techniques – Information security management system requirements

- ISO/IEC 27002:2005 Information technology – Security techniques – Code of practice for information security management

- ISO/IEC 27003:2010 Information technology – Security techniques – ISMS implementation guidance

- NIST FIPS Pub 200 Minimum Security Requirements for Federal Information and Information Systems

- NIST SP 800-53: Recommended Security Controls for Federal Information Systems

11.3 Risk management

Published

- ISO/IEC 27005:2008 Information technology – Security techniques – ISMS risk management

- ISO/IEC 27003:2010 Information technology – Security techniques – ISMS implementation guidance

- ISO 31000:2009 Risk management – Guidelines on principles and implementation of risk management

- ISO Guide 73 Risk management – Vocabulary – Guidelines for use in standards

- NIST SP 800-30: Risk Management Guide for Information Technology Systems

- NIST SP 800-39: Managing Risk from Information Systems – An Organizational Perspective

- BSI BS 31100:2008 Risk management – Code of practice

- AS/NZS 4360:2004 – Risk Management

Under development

- ISO/IEC 27033 Information technology – Security techniques

  - Part 3 Reference networking scenarios – Risks, design techniques and control issues

  - Part 4 Securing communications between networks using security gateways – Risks, design techniques and control issues

  - Part 5 Securing Virtual Private Networks – Risks, design techniques and control issues

11.4 Information security measurements

Published

- ISO/IEC 27004:2009 Information technology – Security techniques – Information security measurements

- ISO/IEC 27003:2010 Information technology – Security techniques – ISMS Implementation guidance

- Humphreys, T. and Plate, A. (2005) *Measuring the effectiveness of your ISMS implementations based on ISO/IEC 27001 NIST SP 800-55 rev 1: Performance Measurement Guide for Information Security*, British Standards Institution

- NIST Interagency Report 7502 The Common Configuration Scoring System (CCSS)

11.5 ISMS auditing

Published

- ISO/IEC 27006 Information technology – Security techniques – Requirements for bodies providing audit and certification of information security management systems

- ISO 19011 Guidelines for quality and/or environmental management systems auditing

- ISO/PAS 17001:2005 Conformity assessment – Impartiality – Principles and requirements

- ISO 17021:2006 Part 1 Conformance Assessment – Requirements for bodies providing audit and certification of management systems

- Humphreys, T. and Plate, A. (2005) *Guidelines on Requirements and Preparations for ISMS Certification based on ISO/IEC 27001*, British Standards Institution

- Humphreys, T. and Plate, A. (2005) *Are you ready for an ISO/IEC 27001 ISMS audit?*, British Standards Institution

- NIST SP 800-115 Technical Guide to Information Security Testing and Assessment

Under development

- ISO/IEC 27007 Information technology – Security techniques – Guidance for auditors on ISMS controls

- ISO/IEC 27008 Information technology – Security techniques – Guidance for auditors on information security management systems controls

- ISO 17021 Part 2 Conformance Assessment – Requirements for third-party for auditing of management systems

11.6 Training and awareness

Published

- NIST SP 800-50: Building an Information Technology Security Awareness and Training Program

11.7 Incident handling

Published

- ISO/PAS 22399:2007 Incident preparedness and operational continuity management
- NIST SP 800-61 rev 1: Computer Security Incident Handling Guide
- NIST SP 800-86: Guide to Integrating Forensic Techniques into Incident Response
- NIST Handbook for Computer Security Incident Response Teams (CSIRTs)
- RFC-2196: Site Security Handbook – Chapter 5 Security Incident Handling
- The Software Engineering Institute, Carnegie Mellon, Incident Management Capability Metrics
- The Software Engineering Institute, Carnegie Mellon, State of the Practice of Computer Security Incident Response Teams (CSIRTs)

Under development

- ISO/IEC 27035 Information technology – Security techniques – Information security incident management (previously ISO/IEC 18044)

11.8 Services, applications and service management

Published

- ISO/IEC 20000 Part 1 and 2 Service management
- NIST SP 800-35 Guide to Information Technology Security Services

Under development

- ISO/IEC 27031 Information technology – Security techniques – ICT Preparedness for business continuity
- ISO/IEC 27032 Information technology – Security techniques – Guidelines for cybersecurity

- ISO/IEC 27033 Information technology – Security techniques
  - Part 1 Guidelines for network security
  - Part 2 Guidelines for the design and implementation of network security
  - Part 3 Reference networking scenarios – Risks, design techniques and control issues
  - Part 4 Securing communications between networks using security gateways – Risks, design techniques and control issues
  - Part 5 Securing virtual private networks – Risks, design techniques and control issues
  - Part 6 IP convergence
  - Part 7 Guidelines for securing wireless networking – Risks, design techniques and control issues
- ISO/IEC 27034 Information technology – Security techniques
  - Part 1 Application security overview, concepts and principles
  - Part 2 Application security management process
  - Part 3 Architecture, design and development
  - Part 4 Protocols and data structure
  - Part 5 Application security assurance
  - Part 6 Security guidance for specific applications
- ISO/IEC 27035 Information technology – Security techniques – Information security incident management (previously ISO/IEC 18044)
- ISO/IEC 27036 Information technology – Security techniques – Guidelines for the security of outsourcing
- ISO/IEC 27037 Information technology – Security techniques – Guidelines for identification, collection and/or acquisition and preservation of digital evidence

11.9 Business continuity, disaster recovery and ICT preparedness

- BS 25999-1 Business continuity management – Part 1: Code of practice for business continuity management
- BS 25999-2 Business continuity management – Part 2: Specification for business continuity management

- BS 25777 Code of practice for information and communications technology continuity management

- ISO/IEC 24762 Information technology – Security techniques – Guidelines for ICT Disaster recovery services

- ISO/PAS 22399:2007 Incident preparedness and operational continuity management

- Business Continuity Institute (www.thebci.org): A Management Guide to Implementing Global Good Practice in Business Continuity Management

  - Section 1 BCM policy and programme management

  - Section 2 Understanding the organization

  - Section 3 Determining BCM strategy

  - Section 4 Developing and implementing a BCM

  - Section 5 Exercising, maintaining and reviewing BCM arrangements

  - Section 6 Embedding BCM in the organization's culture

- NIST SP 800-34: Contingency Planning for Information Technology Systems

Under development

- ISO/IEC 27031 Information technology – Security techniques – ICT Preparedness for Business Continuity

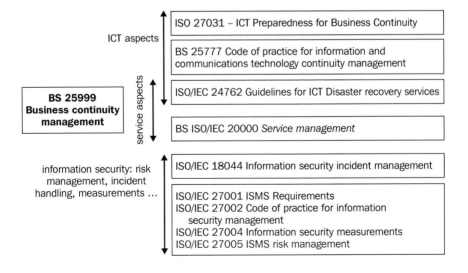

11.10 Harmonization of management system standards

Harmonized management system standards

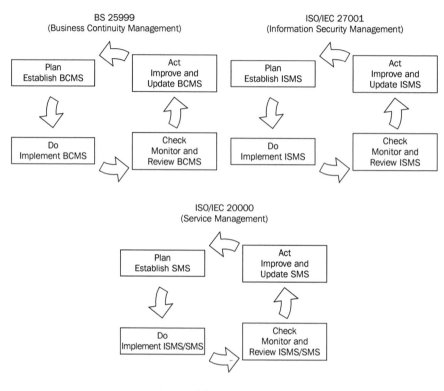

Integrated documentation system
opportunity for integrated audits
integrated risk assessment, asset
management, incident handling
management system, etc.

Annex A Definitions

The following terms and definitions apply through this book.

Control

A measure that is modifying risk [ISO Guide 73:2009]

NOTE 1 Controls include any process, policy, device, practice, or other actions, which modify risk.

NOTE 2 Controls may not always exert the intended or assumed modifying effect.

Event

An occurrence or change of a particular set of circumstances [ISO Guide 73:2009]

NOTE 1 An event can be one or more occurrences, and can have several causes.

NOTE 2 An event can consist of something not happening.

NOTE 3 An event can sometimes be referred to as an 'incident' or 'accident'.

NOTE 4 An event without consequences can also be referred to as a 'near miss', 'incident', 'near hit' or 'close call'.

Information security effectiveness

This is a measure of how well the ISMS processes are performing and how they achieve the organization's objectives and requirements, or a measure of one or more controls that are implemented in the ISMS, indicating whether they achieve their identified information security objectives and risk reduction [BSI BIP 074].

Information security event

An information security event is an identified occurrence of a system, service or network state indicating a possible breach of information security policy or failure of safeguards, or a previously unknown situation that may be security relevant [ISO/IEC TR 18044:2004].

Information security incident

An information security incident is indicated by a single or a series of unwanted or unexpected information security events that have a significant probability of compromising business operations and threatening information security [ISO/IEC TR 18044:2004].

Information security indicators

These are used to indicate the state or level of something being measured, for example, how well the currently deployed information security processes or controls meet information security policy and objectives [BSI BIP 074].

Information security risk

Effect of uncertainty on information security objectives [ISO/IEC 27000]

NOTE 1 For information security risks an effect is a deviation from the expected, and is always negative.

NOTE 2 Information security risk is associated with the potential that a given threat will exploit vulnerabilities of an asset or group of assets and thereby cause harm to an organization.

NOTE 3 Risk is often characterized by reference to potential events and consequences, or a combination of these.

NOTE 4 Risk is often expressed in terms of a combination of the consequences of an event (including changes in circumstances) and the associated likelihood of occurrence.

NOTE 5 Uncertainty is the state, even partial, of deficiency of information related to understanding or knowledge of an event, its consequence, or likelihood.

Likelihood	The state or fact of something being likely. In non-technical parlance, 'likelihood' is usually a synonym for 'probability', but in mathematical and statistical usage there is a clear distinction: whereas 'probability' allows us to predict unknown outcomes based on known parameters, 'likelihood' allows us to estimate unknown parameters based on known outcomes.
Metric	A metric defines a system or standard of measurement, for example, the metric system that is used to measure length, capacity and weights or mass. Metrics defined for information security purposes serve a similar purpose; they provide standard scales and units of measurement against which the effectiveness and/or performance of information security arrangements can be measured. Although there are several metrics published (e.g. on the internet), it is best that organizations define their own metrics, suitable for their requirements and needs [BSI BIP 074].
Measure	A measure is a means of ascertaining the size, amount or degree of (something) by comparison with a standard unit or with an object of known size; i.e. to assess the amount, degree, extent or quality of something against a standard scale (which can be defined by the metric, see above) [BSI BIP 074].
Measurement	A measurement is the action of measuring to determine an amount, size, extent, degree or quality; the scale that is needed for this measurement is defined by the corresponding metric (see above). Continuing the simple example above, the measurement gives the results of the measuring activities, e.g. a length of 2 m or a height of 0.5 m.

Measurement *(continued)*	Measurements for information security purposes can be used to assess the performance, effectiveness or whatever else an organization might want to measure using the metrics that have been defined [BSI BIP 074].
Residual risk	The risk remaining after risk treatment [ISO Guide 73:2009]
	NOTE 1 Residual risk can contain unidentified risk.
	NOTE 2 Residual risk is also known as 'retained risk'.
Risk	A combination of the probability of an event and its consequence [ISO Guide 73:2009]
Risk acceptance	A decision to accept a risk [ISO Guide 73:2009]
	NOTE 1 The verb 'to accept' is chosen to convey the idea that acceptance has its basic dictionary meaning.
	NOTE 2 Risk acceptance depends on risk criteria.
Risk analysis	A systematic use of information to identify sources and to estimate the risk [ISO Guide 73:2009]
	NOTE 1 Risk analysis provides a basis for risk evaluation, risk treatment, and risk acceptance.
	NOTE 2 Information can include historical data, theoretical analysis, informed opinions, and the concerns of stakeholders.
Risk assessment	The overall process of risk analysis and risk evaluation [ISO Guide 73:2009]
Risk avoidance	The decision not to become involved in, or action to withdraw from, a risk situation
	NOTE The decision may be taken based on the result of risk evaluation.

Risk communication	The exchange or sharing of information about risk between the decision maker and other stakeholders [ISO Guide 73:2009] *NOTE The information can relate to the existence, nature, form, probability, severity, acceptability, treatment or other aspects of risk.*
Risk control	Actions implementing risk management decisions [ISO Guide 73:2009] *NOTE Risk control may involve monitoring, re-evaluation, and compliance with decisions.*
Risk criteria	Terms of reference by which the significance of risk is assessed [ISO Guide 73:2009] *NOTE Risk criteria can include associated cost and benefits, legal and statutory requirements, socio-economic and environmental aspects, the concerns of stakeholders, priorities and other inputs to the assessment.*
Risk evaluation	A process of comparing the estimated risk against given risk criteria to determine the significance of risk [ISO Guide 73:2009]
Risk identification	Process of finding, recognizing and describing risks [ISO Guide 73:2009] *NOTE 1 Risk identification involves the identification of risk sources, events, their causes and their potential consequences.* *NOTE 2 Risk identification can involve historical data, theoretical analysis, informed and expert opinions, and stakeholders' needs.*
Risk management	Co-ordinated activities to direct and control an organization with regard to risk [ISO Guide 73:2009] *NOTE Risk management generally includes risk assessment, risk treatment, risk acceptance and risk communication.*

Risk management system	A set of elements of an organization's management system concerned with managing risk [ISO Guide 73:2009]

NOTE 1 Management system elements can include strategic planning, decision making and other processes for dealing with risk.

NOTE 2 The culture of an organization is reflected in its risk management system.

Risk reduction	Actions taken to lessen the probability, negative consequences, or both, associated with a risk

Risk transfer	Sharing with another party the burden of loss or benefit of gain, for a risk

NOTE 1 Legal or statutory requirements can limit, prohibit or mandate the transfer of certain risk.

NOTE 2 Risk transfer can be carried out through insurance or other agreements.

NOTE 3 Risk transfer can create new risks or modify existing risk.

NOTE 4 Relocation of the source is not risk transfer.

Risk treatment	A treatment process of selection and implementation of measures to modify risk [ISO Guide 73:2009]

NOTE 1 Risk treatment can involve:

- *avoiding the risk by deciding not to start or continue with the activity that gives rise to the risk;*

- *taking or increasing risk in order to pursue an opportunity;*

- *removing the risk source;*

- *changing the likelihood;*

- *changing the consequences;*

- *sharing the risk with another party or parties (including contracts and risk financing); and*

- *retaining the risk by informed choice.*

Risk treatment *(continued)*

NOTE 2 Risk treatments that deal with negative consequences are sometimes referred to as 'risk mitigation', 'risk elimination', 'risk prevention' and 'risk reduction'.

NOTE 3 Risk treatment can create new risks or modify existing risks.

Threat

A potential cause of an incident that may result in harm to a system or organization

Vulnerability

A weakness of an asset or group of assets that can be exploited by one or more threats

Annex B Examples of legal and regulatory compliance

B.1 General

Organizations increasingly face the need to comply with a range of legislation and regulation that has an impact on their management of information. There are four main drivers for this.

- Corporate governance – for example, as a result of high-profile organizational failures of corporate governance

- Electronic commerce – for example, as a result of the need to ensure the development of trust in online trading

- National infrastructure security – for example, as a result of the increase in global terrorism

- Identity theft and data protection/privacy. This is as a result of apparent lapses in corporate security that have resulted in exposing consumers to identity theft or caused data protection problems

Other drivers include health and safety, making provision for employees and customers with disabilities, intellectual property, the need to protect tax revenue and the need to avoid discrimination in employment. The intention of such legislation and regulation is to ensure that organizations put in place effective mechanisms for controlling and auditing the flow of information (personal, financial and operational). Most legislation and regulation of this kind also sees risk assessment as an essential element of these effective control mechanisms.

B.1.1 Legal framework

Making sense of the increasing number of legal and regulatory instruments requires a clear framework that reflects and simplifies their main purpose. For this reason, legal and regulatory instruments are considered as falling into one of six groups based on shared functionality. The first four groups result from the drivers mentioned earlier in this annex:

- corporate governance;

- electronic commerce and the civil and criminal legal framework;

- national infrastructure security;

- identity theft and data protection/privacy;

- the other two groups deal with legislation and regulation that relates to

    - intellectual property protection; and

    - sector (industry)-specific provisions.

In this annex each of these groups is explained in more detail, and examples are given of appropriate legislation and regulations from Europe and North America, as these are the instruments that are of primary interest to UK organizations (although such changes are occurring worldwide and should be monitored, if of interest).

B.2 Corporate governance

B.2.1 General

Legislation and regulation in this area is primarily directed at publicly traded companies, requiring them to demonstrate due diligence in the disclosure of financial information, to manage their operational risk transparently and to implement a series of internal controls and procedures that will enable them to do so [20]. The intent here is to assure potential and current investors that they can justifiably rely on the records of the business to present a true picture of the organization.

B.2.2 Europe

In Europe corporate governance has, in general, been seen as an issue that is dealt with through regulations such as the Combined Code for Internal Control (Turnbull) [3], for companies quoted on the London Stock Exchange (LSE); the Basel II operation risk control provisions for banks that trade internationally; and the *Financial Services Authority (FSA) Handbook* for banks and financial services organizations in the UK [4]. However, control of audit processes has become part of statutory law in the UK with the Companies (Audit, Investigation and Community Enterprise) Act 2004 [5]. The intent of the legislation and regulation is to assure potential and current investors that they can rely on published financial statements of the business to present a true picture.

B.2.3 North America

In the USA the Sarbanes-Oxley Act (SOX) [6] has put corporate governance onto a strong statutory footing by holding corporate officers personally liable for improprieties, with penalties of imprisonment for CEOs and CFOs in the event of non-compliance.

B.3 Electronic commerce, legal framework

B.3.1 General

The legislation under this heading is that which is intended to govern the use of information technology and networked systems, particularly in order to increase trust in online transactions. For example:

- use of electronic records and electronic signatures;

- the creation, modification, storage and transmission of electronic data; and

- criminal misuse of computers and IT systems.

B.3.2 Europe

Most countries in Europe have an equivalent of the UK's Computer Misuse Act 1990 [7]. The EU has been active in considering the legal framework in this area and examples include:

- Electronic Signatures Directive [8];

- Consumer Protection and Distance Selling Directive [9];

- Directive on Privacy and Electronic Communications [10];

- Council of Europe, Convention on CyberCrime.

B.3.3 North America

The USA has been less active in this area. Implementation has been sector-specific – for example, the Food and Drug Administration (FDA) provisions governing the use of Electronic Records and Signatures in the pharmaceutical industry (21CFR11) [11]. The Securities and Exchange Commission (SEC) has been active in the area of document life cycle management and has proffered US federal regulations, which have also been adopted by several states.

B.4 National infrastructure security

B.4.1 General

National security provisions are intended to protect citizens from threats to the critical national infrastructure arising from perils such as terrorism (however motivated), state-sponsored intervention, or natural disaster.

B.4.2 Europe

European provisions in this area tend not to involve statutory instruments. Most governments have an agency, or agencies, that are tasked with the protection of the critical national information infrastructure (such as the Network Infrastructure Security Co-ordination Centre (NISCC) in the UK). In 2004 the EU set up the European Network Information Security Agency (ENISA).

B.4.3 North America

The USA has given the Department of Homeland Security (DHS) overall responsibility for protecting the critical national infrastructure, and has implemented a number of statutory instruments, and given industry organizations or government agencies responsibility for dealing with some aspects of the task. These include:

- Federal Information Security Management Act (FISMA) [1];
- USA Patriot Act (USAPA) [2];
- North American Electric Reliability Council;
- Federal Energy Regulatory Commission.

B.5 Identity theft and data protection/privacy

B.5.1 General

Instruments in this area are intended to identify the rights and obligations of individuals and organizations with respect to the collection, use, retention and disclosure of personal information.

Notification in the event of inappropriate disclosure is required.

NOTE: SOX applies to any company that is publicly-listed in the USA, which may include companies headquartered elsewhere.

B.5.2 Europe

In the European Union all countries have implemented national legislation on the basis of the European Union Data Protection Directive [12].

B.5.3 North America

Canada has adopted an approach similar to that of the European Union with the Personal Information Protection and Electronic Document Act (PIPEDA) [13].

In the USA a piecemeal approach has been adopted. Privacy legislation has been directed at specific areas, such as:

- Gramm-Leach-Bliley Act (GLBA) [14];

- Health Insurance Portability and Accountability Act (HIPAA) [15].

Or it has been targeted at specific types of crime, for example:

- California Security Breach Information Act (Senate Bill No. 1386) (targeted at identity theft) [16];

- Children's Online Privacy Protection Act (COPPA) [17];

- Family Educational Rights and Privacy Act (FERPA) [18].

There is also the EU–USA Safe Harbor Agreement [21].

B.6 Intellectual property protection

Legislation under this heading is intended to protect the intellectual property of individuals and organizations, such as trade secrets and patentable ideas. All countries have some form of trade secret, copyright and patent law.

B.7 Sector-specific

Sector-specific regulations are those targeted at specific industries, intended to control aspects of their operation that are unique to that sector and that might impinge on their security, or the security of the wider public. Examples include the FDA provisions for pharmaceutical companies and data retention laws that affect telecommunications providers and ISPs. The regulations applicable to credit card companies also apply to organizations dealing with these companies.

Sector-specific regulations are very important to many organizations but, because they are so widely varied, they are not discussed in detail here. Organizations should determine which sector-specific regulations are relevant in the jurisdictions in which they operate, and factor them into their risk evaluations.

Annex C Examples of assets, threats, vulnerabilities and risk assessment methods

C.1 Asset identification

One of the most valuable and important types of asset is information, and information needs to be protected irrespective of the form it takes. For example, information needs to be protected whether it is in databases and data files, company or system documentation, contracts, user manuals, training material, operational or support procedures, guidelines, documents containing important business results, continuity plans, or fallback arrangements.

In addition, there are other assets that are used to store or process information, or have an impact on the security of the information assets. These other assets include the following:

- *Processes and services:* including business processes, application specific activities, computing and communications services and other technical services supporting the processing of information (heating, lighting, power, air-conditioning services);

- *Software:* including application software, system software, development tools and utilities;

- *Physical items:* including computer and communications equipment, media (paper, tapes, CDs and disks), and other technical equipment (power supplies, air-conditioning units), furniture and accommodation that are used to support the processing of information;

- *People:* including personnel, customers, subscribers, and any other person within the ISMS that is involved with storing or processing information.

For a comprehensive assessment, it is also important to identify organizational assets that might be influenced by information security, such as the organization's image and reputation.

C.2 Types of asset

The organization, its image and reputation and its business needs and requirements, people working in the organization and with the information, services, media, IT and software that is used to store or process the information are typical types of asset.

C.3 Example list of threats

The following list provides some examples of the threats and vulnerabilities associated with the ISO/IEC 27001:2005 control objectives and controls. This is not an exhaustive list of threats and vulnerabilities and they should only be taken as examples to illustrate the concepts and the relationship with the controls given in ISO/IEC 27001:2005.

Again the most important principle is that an organization needs to adopt risk assessment and risk management approaches that will appropriately address and identify the complete range of threats and vulnerabilities relevant to its business environment, which could include some or all of the threats and vulnerabilities given in the following list.

The following is an example list of threats derived from selected parts of ISO/IEC 27001:2005. This list of threats is presented here for illustrative purposes and should not be taken as being definitive and complete:

- acts of terrorism;
- air conditioning failure;
- airborne particles/dust;
- bomb attack;
- breach of legislation or regulations;
- breaches of contractual obligations;
- compromise of assets;
- compromise of security;
- damage caused by penetration tests;
- damage caused by third parties;
- destruction of records;
- destruction of the business continuity plans;
- deterioration of media;
- disasters (natural or man-made);
- disclosure of information;
- disclosure of passwords;
- disruption to business processes;
- dust;
- earthquake;
- eavesdropping;
- environmental contamination (and other forms of natural or man-made disasters);
- equipment failure;
- errors;
- failure of communications services;
- failure of supporting utilities (such as electricity, water supply, sewage, heating, ventilation, and air-conditioning)

- falsification of records;
- fire;
- flooding;
- fraud;
- hardware failure;
- hurricanes;
- illegal import/export of software;
- illegal use of software;
- industrial action;
- information leakage;
- information security incidents;
- interception;
- interference;
- interruption to business activities and processes;
- introduction of unauthorized or untested code;
- lightning;
- loss of integrity;
- loss of records;
- loss of service;
- maintenance error;
- malfunctions of supporting utilities;
- malicious code;
- masquerading of user identity;
- misuse of audit tools;
- misuse of information processing facilities;
- misuse of resources or assets;
- network access by unauthorized persons;
- operational support staff error;
- power fluctuation;
- security failure;
- software failure;
- system failure;
- system misuse (accidental or deliberate);
- theft;
- tornadoes
- unauthorized access;
- unauthorized access to audit logs;
- unauthorized access to audit tools;
- unauthorized modification of audit logs;
- unauthorized or unintentional modification;
- unauthorized physical access;
- unauthorized use of IPR material;
- unauthorized use of software;
- unavailability;
- unsuccessful changes;
- use of network facilities in an unauthorized way;
- use of software by unauthorized users;
- use of software in an unauthorized way;
- user error;
- vandalism;
- violation of intellectual property rights;
- wilful damage.

Depending on the type of threat, its occurrence could result in a number of different outcomes, such as:

- accidental or unintended changes to software and data-sharing facilities in a computing environment;

- breach of security as a result of non-compliance with operational procedures;

- breach of security as a result of inaccurate, incomplete or inappropriate operating procedures or the definition of responsibilities, or insufficient updating of such procedures;

- breach of security as a result of non-compliance with incident handling procedures;

- compromise, damage or loss of data at a contractor's site;

- damage caused by inaccurate, incomplete or inappropriate continuity plans, insufficient testing or insufficient updating of plans;

- denial of service, system resources, information;

- email bombs;

- forgery;

- fraud;

- negligent or deliberate misuse of facilities as a result of lack of segregation and execution of duties;

- unauthorized disclosure of the location of sites/buildings/offices containing critical and/or sensitive computing and processing facilities;

- unauthorized disclosure of information.

C.4 Threat examples and ISO/IEC 27001:2005

The following illustrates by example how the various threats given earlier in this annex relate to selected control objectives given in ISO/IEC 27002:2005.

C.4.1 Physical and environmental security

Secure areas

Objective: To prevent unauthorized physical access, damage, and interference to the organization's premises and information. Critical or sensitive information processing facilities should be housed in secure areas, protected by defined security perimeters, with appropriate security barriers and entry controls.

NOTE This corresponds to ISO/IEC 27001:2005, Annex A.9.1.

The following threats relate to this objective:

- bomb attack;
- earthquake;
- environmental contamination (and other forms of natural or man-made disasters);
- fire;
- flooding;
- hurricane;
- industrial action;
- interference;
- theft;
- unauthorized physical access;
- wilful damage.

Equipment security

Objective: To prevent loss, damage, theft or compromise of assets and interruption to the organization's activities. Equipment should be protected from physical and environmental threats.

NOTE This corresponds to ISO/IEC 27001:2005, Annex A.9.2.

The following threats relate to this objective:

- airborne particles/dust;
- air conditioning failure;
- bomb attack;
- dust;
- environmental contamination (and other forms of natural or man-made disasters);
- eavesdropping;
- failure of supporting utilities (such as electricity, water supply, sewage, heating, ventilation, and air-conditioning);
- fire;
- flooding;
- hardware failure;
- information leakage;
- interception;
- interference;
- interruption of activities;
- lightning;
- maintenance errors;
- malfunctions of supporting utilities;
- malicious code;
- power fluctuation;
- theft;
- unauthorized physical access;
- vandalism;
- wilful damage.

C.4.2 Communications and operations management

Operational procedures and responsibilities

Objective: To ensure the correct and secure operation of information processing facilities. Responsibilities and procedures for the management and operation of all information processing facilities should be established.

NOTE This corresponds to ISO/IEC 27001:2005, Annex A.10.1

The following threats relate to this objective:

- disclosure of information;
- theft of information;
- unauthorized access;
- unauthorized or unintentional modification;
- unauthorized changes to operational systems;
- unsuccessful changes to operational systems;
- fraud;
- scams;
- social engineering attacks;
- introduction of unauthorized or untested code;
- attack by malicious code;
- masquerading of user identity;
- misuse of resources or assets;
- operational support staff error;
- software failure;
- system misuse (accidental or deliberate);
- system failures, overloads and downtimes;
- use of software by unauthorized users;
- use of software in an unauthorized way;
- user errors, mistakes, bad judgements;
- wilful damage or harm to operational systems.

Information security aspects of business continuity management

Objective: To counteract interruptions to business activities and to protect critical business processes from the effects of major failures of information systems or disasters and to ensure their timely resumption.

A business continuity management process should be implemented to minimize the impact on the organization and recover from loss of information assets.

NOTE This corresponds to ISO/IEC 27001:2005, Annex A.14.1.

The following threats relate to this objective:

- acts of terrorism;

- disasters (natural or man-made);

- destruction of the business continuity plans;

- errors;

- equipment failure;

- fire;

- information security incidents;

- interruption to business activities and processes;

- lack of business continuity tests;

- lack of reviews and updating of business continuity plans;

- loss of services;

- security failures;

- system failures;

- threats to the environment;

- threats to operational systems;

- threats to communication systems;

- unavailability.

C.4.3 Compliance

Compliance with legal requirements

Objective: To avoid breaches of any law, statutory, regulatory or contractual obligation, and of any security requirement. The design, operation, use and management of information systems may be subject to statutory, regulatory, and contractual security requirements.

NOTE *This corresponds to ISO/IEC 27001:2005, Annex A.15.*

The following threats relate to this objective:

- breaches of contractual obligations;

- breach of legislation or regulations;

- destruction of records;

- deterioration of archived material and the media used for archiving;

- falsification of records;

- illegal import/export of software;

- illegal use of software;

- loss of records;

- misuse of information processing facilities;

- unauthorized access;

- unauthorized use of IPR material;

- unauthorized use of software;

- use of network facilities in an unauthorized way;

- violation of intellectual property rights.

Compliance with security policies and standards, and technical compliance

Objective: To ensure compliance of systems with organizational security policies and standards. The security of information systems should be regularly reviewed.

NOTE *This corresponds to ISO/IEC 27001:2005, Annex A.15.2.*

The following threats relate to this objective:

- compromise of security policy;

- damage caused by penetration tests;

- failure of communications services;

- misuse of resources;

- network access by unauthorized persons;

- illegal import/export of software;
- illegal use of software;
- malicious code;
- theft;
- unauthorized access;
- unauthorized use of software;
- use of network facilities in an unauthorized way;
- wilful damage.

Information systems audit considerations

Objective: To maximize the effectiveness of, and to minimize interference to or from, the information systems audit process. There should be controls to safeguard operational systems and audit tools during information systems audits.

NOTE This corresponds to ISO/IEC 27001:2005, Annex A.15.3.

The following threats relate to this objective:

- damage caused by third parties;
- disclosure of passwords;
- disruption to business processes;
- interference to or from the audit process;
- loss of integrity;
- misuse of audit tools;
- unauthorized access to audit logs;
- unauthorized access to audit tools;
- unauthorized modification of audit logs.

C.5 Vulnerability examples and ISO/IEC 27001:2005

The following lists give examples of vulnerabilities in various security areas, including examples of threats which might exploit these vulnerabilities. The lists can provide help during the assessment of vulnerabilities. It is emphasized that other threats could also exploit these vulnerabilities.

Human resources security (ISO/IEC 27001:2005, Annex A.8)

The vulnerability could be:

- insufficient user training and awareness;
- lack of operational support;
- lack of security awareness – user errors;
- lack of monitoring mechanisms – use of software in an unauthorized way;
- lack of policies for the correct use of telecommunications media and messaging – use of network facilities in an unauthorized way;
- no removal of access rights upon job termination – unauthorized access;
- no procedure to ensure return of asset upon job termination – theft;
- unmotivated or disgruntled staff – misuse of information processing facilities;
- unsupervised work by outside staff or staff working outside normal business hours – theft;
- user errors.

Physical and environmental security (ISO/IEC 27001:2005, Annex A.9)

The vulnerability could be:

- inadequate or careless use of physical access control to buildings, rooms and offices;
- wilful damage;
- lack of physical protection for the building, doors, and windows – theft;
- location in an area susceptible to flooding;
- unprotected storage – theft;
- insufficient maintenance/faulty installation of storage media – maintenance errors;
- lack of periodic equipment replacement schemes – deterioration of storage media;
- susceptibility of equipment to humidity, dust, soiling, airborne particles/dust;
- susceptibility of equipment to temperature variations and extremes of temperature;
- susceptibility of equipment to voltage variations and power fluctuation;
- unstable power grid power fluctuation.

*Communications and operations management
(ISO/IEC 27001:2005, Annex A.10)*

The vulnerability could be:

- complicated user interface – operational staff error;
- disposal or reuse of storage media without proper erasure – unauthorized access to information;
- inadequate change control – security failure;
- inadequate network management – traffic overloading;
- lack of backup procedures – loss of information;
- lack of proof of sending or receiving a message – repudiation;
- lack of updates for malicious code protection – software virus infection;
- no segregation of duties – system misuse (accidental or deliberate);
- no separation of test and operational facilities – unauthorized modification of operational systems;
- uncontrolled copying – theft;
- unprotected public network connections – use of software by unauthorized users.

Access control (ISO/IEC 27001:2005, Annex A.11)

The vulnerability could be:

- inappropriate segregation of networks – unauthorized connections in networks;
- lack of clear desk and clear screen policy – loss of or damage to information;
- lack of identification and authentication mechanisms such as user authentication – masquerading of user identity;
- lack of protection of mobile computing equipment – unauthorized access to information;
- no, or incorrect, access control policy – unauthorized access to information, systems or software;
- no 'logout' when leaving the workstation – use of software by unauthorized users;
- no, or insufficient, software testing – use of software by unauthorized users;
- no review of user access rights – access by users who have left the organization or changed jobs;

- poor password management (easily guessable passwords, storing of passwords, insufficient frequency of change) – masquerading of user identity;

- default factory accounts and passwords are not disabled or changed – unauthorized access to information, systems or software;

- uncontrolled use of system utilities overriding system or application controls.

Information systems acquisition, development and maintenance (ISO/IEC 27001:2005, Annex A.12)

The vulnerability could be:

- inappropriate protection of cryptographic keys – disclosure of information;

- incomplete policy on the use of cryptography – breach of legislation or regulations;

- lack of control of input or output – data error;

- lack of validation of processed data – corruption of information;

- no, or insufficient, software testing – use of software by unauthorized users;

- poorly documented software – operational support staff error;

- unclear or incomplete specifications for developers – software failure;

- uncontrolled downloading and using software, malicious software;

- uncontrolled use of shareware/freeware for corporate applications;

- legal liability;

- well known flaws in the software – use of software by unauthorized users;

- incorrect selection of test data – unauthorized access to personal data.

Annex D Risk management tools

General

A variety of methods exist for undertaking risk assessment and risk management reviews ranging from simple question-and-answer checklist-based approaches (that nonetheless address business risks, and are not mere compliance checklists) through to structured analysis-based techniques.

There are many commercially available tools which can be used to assist the assessment process. These include both automated (computer assisted) and manual products. Whatever methods or products are used by the organization, they should at least address the risk components, relationships between the components, and processes, as described in Chapters 5 and 6.

Once a risk assessment review has been completed for the first time, the results of the review (assets and their values, security requirements and risk levels, and identified controls) should be stored and documented, for example, in a database. Software support tools can make this activity, and any future reassessment activity, much easier.

Another important aspect that should not be overlooked is that users need appropriate training in the use of risk management tools.

Selecting a risk management tool

The following list gives a few ideas of criteria to be considered when selecting a risk assessment tool.

The tool should at least contain modules for:

* data collection;

* analysis;

* output of results.

The method upon which the selected tool works and functions should reflect the organization's policy and overall approach to risk assessment.

Effective reporting of the results of risk assessment is an essential part of the process if management are to weigh the alternatives and make an appropriate, reliable and cost-effective selection of controls. Therefore, the tool should be capable of reporting the results in a clear and accurate manner.

The ability to maintain a history of the information collected during the data collection phase, and of the analysis, is useful in subsequent reviews or queries.

Documentation describing the tool is essential for its effective use and should be available.

The tool selected should be compatible with the hardware and software in use in the organization.

Automated tools are generally efficient and error free, but some can be more difficult to install or learn. It might be necessary, therefore, to consider the availability of training and support for the tool.

The effective use of the tool depends, in part, on how well the user understands the product and whether it has been installed and configured correctly: the availability of guidance on installation and use might be essential.

Bibliography

Legislation

[1] UNITED STATES OF AMERICA. Federal Information Security Management Act of 2002. Washington: Government Printing Office.

[2] UNITED STATES OF AMERICA. Uniting and Strengthening America by Providing Appropriate Tools Required to Intercept and Obstruct Terrorism (USA Patriot Act) Act of 2001. Washington: Government Printing Office.

[5] GREAT BRITAIN. Companies (Audit, Investigation and Community Enterprise) Act 2004. London: The Stationery Office.

[6] UNITED STATES OF AMERICA. Sarbanes-Oxley Act of 2002. Washington: Government Printing Office.

[7] GREAT BRITAIN. Computer Misuse Act 1990. London: The Stationery Office.

[8] EUROPEAN COMMUNITIES. 1999/93/EC. Council Directive of 13 December on a Community Framework for Electronic Signatures. Luxembourg: Office for Official Publications of the European Communities, 1999.

[9] EUROPEAN COMMUNITIES. Directive 97/7/EC of the European Parliament and of the Council of 20 May 1997 on the protection of consumers in respect of distance contracts. Luxembourg: Office for Official Publications of the European Communities, 1997.

[10] EUROPEAN COMMUNITIES. 2002/58/EC. Directive of the European Parliament and of the Council of 12 July 2002 concerning the processing of personal data and the protection of privacy in the electronic communications sector (Directive on privacy and electronic communications). Luxembourg: Office for Official Publications of the European Communities, 2002.

[11] UNITED STATES OF AMERICA. Code of Federal Regulations: Title 21: Food and Drugs, Part 11: Electronic Records, Electronic Signatures (21CFR11). Washington: Government Printing Office.

[12] 95/46/EC. Directive of the European Parliament on the protection of individuals with regard to the processing of personal data and on the free movement of such data. Luxembourg: Office for Official Publications of the European Communities, 1995.

[13] CANADA. Personal Information Protection and Electronic Documents Act 2000.

[14] UNITED STATES OF AMERICA. Gramm-Leach-Bliley Act of 1999. Washington: Government Printing Office.

[15] UNITED STATES OF AMERICA. Health Insurance Portability and Accountability Act of 1996. Washington: Government Printing Office.

[16] UNITED STATES OF AMERICA. California Senate Bill No.1386. California Security Breach Information Act. Washington: Senate Printing and Document Services, 2002.

[17] UNITED STATES OF AMERICA. Children's Online Privacy Protection Act of 1998. Washington: Government Printing Office.

[18] UNITED STATES OF AMERICA. Family Educational Rights and Privacy Act of 1974, as amended. Washington: Government Printing Office.

[21] EU–USA Safe Harbor Agreement regarding compliance by US companies with the EU Directive 95/46/EC on the protection of personal data

Books and articles

[3] The Institute of Chartered Accountants in England and Wales, 2005. *Internal Control: Guidance for Directors on the Combined Code.*

[4] Financial Services Authority. *Financial Services Authority (FSA) Handbook.* London: FSA, 2005.

[19] *OECD Guidelines for the Security of Information Systems and Networks: Towards a Culture of Security,* Paris: OECD, 2002.

[20] *OECD Principles of Corporate Governance,* Paris: OECD, 2004.

[22] E. J. Humphreys, *Implementing the ISO/IEC 27001 Information Security Management System Standard,* Artech House Publishers, (2007)

[23] ISO Publication – *ISO/IEC 27001 Information Security Management Systems: An easy-to-use guide for the small business* (2010)